I0420371

CONTENTS

Preparation Manual for the U.S. Border Patrol Entrance Examination

INTRODUCTION

Purpose of the Manual

The purpose of this manual is to help you prepare to take the U.S. Border Patrol Entrance Examination. This manual will familiarize you with the U.S. Border Patrol Logical Reasoning Test, the Spanish Language Proficiency Test, and the Artificial Language Test (ALT) and will give you a chance to study some sample questions and explanations for the correct answers to each question. If you have not had much practice taking written, multiple-choice tests, you will have an opportunity to see what the tests look like and to practice taking questions similar to those on the tests.

Organization of the Manual

The manual is organized into four sections. The first section provides some tips for taking the U.S. Border Patrol Entrance Examination. The second section provides preparation material for the U.S. Border Patrol Logical Reasoning Test and a practice test with explanations for the answers to the practice test. Sample questions for the Spanish Language Proficiency Test follow in the third section. The final section provides a practice test for the ALT along with explanations for the answers to the practice test.

Section I: Test Taking Tips

1. You will do your best on the test if you stay calm and relaxed. Take a few deep, slow breaths to help you maintain your calm.

2. Pay careful attention to all directions before beginning.

3. Answer the easier questions first. Skip questions you find to be very difficult and come back to them later.

4. For each question, read the entire question and all response options carefully before deciding upon an answer.

5. If you do not know the answer to a question, eliminate the response options that you know to be incorrect or probably incorrect and then guess from the remaining response options.

6. Your score is based only on the number of questions you answer correctly. You are not penalized for answering questions incorrectly. Therefore, you should answer every question, even questions that you must guess.

7. If you finish before time is up, go back and check your answers.

8. Be sure that you mark your answer sheet correctly. If you have to change an answer, erase the first answer before marking the new answer. If you skip a question, be sure to answer the next question in the appropriate place on the answer sheet.

9. Ignore any patterns of A's, B's, C's, D's, or E's on your answer sheet. These correct answer positions are chosen randomly and there is no way to improve your chances by guessing based on an answer sheet pattern.

10. Take the Spanish Language Proficiency Test if you are proficient in standard Spanish; otherwise take the Artificial Language Test.

Section II. Preparing for the U.S. Border Patrol Logical Reasoning Test

INTRODUCTION

Purpose of this Section

The purpose of this section is to help you prepare to take the U.S. Border Patrol Logical Reasoning Test. The test described in this section evaluates how well applicants can read, understand, and apply critical thinking skills to factual situations. Border Patrol Agents must read and study laws, legal commentary, and regulations. They often must make critical decisions that require superior reasoning skills. Additionally, they may be called upon to testify in court and must be able to follow and anticipate the kind of reasoning used in legal proceedings. As a result, they will receive training at the Border Patrol Academy that requires that they read, understand, and be able to apply a wealth of detailed, written information. Although some information must be memorized, much of the information that Border Patrol Agents will use must be learned through independent reasoning. This test is designed to select trainees who will be able to handle the very demanding academic workload at the Border Patrol Academy and who will subsequently be able to handle complex reasoning and decision-making situations on the job.

This section of the manual will familiarize you with the test and the instructions and will give you a chance to study some sample questions and explanations for the correct answers to each question. You will have an opportunity to see what the test looks like and to practice taking questions similar to those on the test.

Organization of this Section

Section II is organized into two parts. The first part explains the types of questions on the test. The practice test follows in the second part. It contains questions that are similar to, but not exactly the same as, the questions on the real test. The practice test is followed by detailed explanations of every practice test question. These explanations will give you information about what is correct about the correct response options and what is incorrect about the wrong response options. Understanding the reasons for the correct and incorrect response options should assist you in distinguishing between a right and wrong answer on the test.

Educated Guessing

There is no penalty for guessing on this test; therefore, you should answer every question. If you guess blindly, you have one chance in five of getting the right answer. However, your chance of choosing the right answer just by guessing is greatly improved by using a little mental detective work to eliminate one or more response options that are probably or certainly wrong.

A poor guessing strategy is to try to determine the next answer based on its letter or on some pattern of letters among the answer choices. There may be several D's or A's or any other letter in a row, or there may not be. Trying to uncover some pattern in these letters and guessing based on that pattern is not an effective test-taking strategy.

PREPARING FOR LOGICAL REASONING QUESTIONS

Logical Reasoning

Reasoning is the single most important competency for successful performance in Border Patrol jobs (and in other jobs in the economy). Correct reasoning is useful for decision making and problem solving, activities that prevail on the job. In this part, you will read some useful information about reasoning correctly.

The questions in this examination are designed to test your ability to understand complicated written material and to derive correct conclusions from it. The kind of reading that these questions ask you to do is different from ordinary reading in which you just follow the general meaning of a series of sentences to see what the writer thinks about a topic. It is the kind of reading you have to do with complex material when you intend to take some action or draw some conclusion based on that material.

The test asks you to make logical conclusions based on facts you are given in various paragraphs. These conclusions need to be based only on the facts in the paragraph. Therefore, answering requires careful reading and focused thought about what information is given and what information is <u>not</u> given.

The following information will give you some suggestions about how to approach the questions and some information about how you can develop your reasoning skills.

Reading the Paragraph

Every reading paragraph in the test is drawn from some kind of written material relating to Border Patrol or government work. There may be facts in a paragraph that do not actually apply to every part of the Federal Government or that may not always be true everywhere. In answering the questions, it is important that you **accept every fact in the paragraph as true**. Remember that you are not being judged on your knowledge of facts, but rather on your ability to read and reason on the basis of given facts.

Not all information is the same kind of information. There can be information about events or situations, and there can be information about individuals and groups (or categories). It is important to examine information in the paragraph closely to determine what kind of information it is. Is the information about two or more categories of things? Is the information about how two events or situations are linked together? It is also important to recognize whether the information is positive or negative. Usually, information is positive (for example, "these tire tracks are several days old"), but knowledge that something is <u>not</u> the case is also useful information (for example, "these tire tracks are <u>not</u> from a truck").

Reading the Lead-In or Basic Question

In this test, you will find a paragraph, followed by a lead-in phrase that asks you to complete a sentence by choosing one of several response options labeled from (A) to (E). The lead-in phrase may be either positive or negative: *"From the information given above, it can be validly concluded that"* or *"From the information given above, it CANNOT be validly concluded that."* It is important to focus on the lead-in phrase at the beginning of a question to determine whether it is positive or negative. Do not skim over the lead-in phrase.

Positive lead-in phrases are followed by four invalid conclusions and one valid conclusion. Your task is to find the valid one. Negative lead-in phrases, by contrast, are followed by four valid conclusions and only one invalid conclusion. The task in these questions is to determine what **cannot** be validly concluded based on the facts in the paragraph.

The lead-in phrase may also limit the possible answers in some way. For example, a lead-in phrase such as *"From the information given above, it can be validly concluded that, during the 1990's in California"* means that there might be different answers based on other times and places, but for the purpose of the test question, only conditions in California during the 1990's (as described in the paragraph) should be considered.

Reasoning About Groups or Categories

As was stated before, not all information is the same kind of information. There can be information about events or situations, and there can be information about individuals and groups (or categories). This part of Section II discusses how to deal with information about groups or categories.

"All" Statements

A statement about two groups that begins with the words "all" or "every" gives you some important information about how the two groups are related. The words "all" and "every" tell you that everything in the first group is also in the second group. For example, in the statement, "All the law enforcement officers on the case are Federal law enforcement officers," the first group, consisting of law enforcement officers on the case, is totally included in the second group, consisting of Federal law enforcement officers.

The "all" statement does not provide sufficient information to determine whether or not all members of the second group are included in the first group. Suppose that a librarian told you "All the books on this set of shelves are about law enforcement." From this information, you might be tempted to conclude that all of the library's books on law enforcement (the second group) are on that set of shelves (the first group), but this conclusion is invalid. The books on those shelves might only be part of the entire group of books on law enforcement. The sentence does NOT provide information on whether or not other law enforcement books are placed elsewhere in the library. The following examples provide an "all" statement (all of Group A are Group B) followed by an invalid "all" statement (all of Group B are Group A). To develop a good grasp of this concept, try to create some examples of your own.

| True: | All the people at my party speak Spanish. |
| Therefore, Invalid: | All the people who speak Spanish are at my party. |

| True: | All Supreme Court justices are lawyers. |
| Therefore, Invalid: | All lawyers are Supreme Court justices. |

| True: | All U.S. Presidents were elected. |
| Therefore, Invalid: | All officials who were elected are U.S. Presidents. |

| True: | Every U.S. Border Patrol Agent works for the U.S. Government. |
| Therefore, Invalid: | Everyone working for the U.S. Government is a U.S. Border Patrol Agent. |

| True: | Every U.S. Senator is a member of the U.S. Congress. |
| Therefore, Invalid: | Every member of the U.S. Congress is a U.S. Senator. |

Every "all" statement provides sufficient information to determine that at least some members of the second group are included in the first group. Returning to our previous examples, we can validly conclude that "some Federal law enforcement officers are on the case" and that "some of the books about law enforcement are on this set of shelves." Developing numerous examples on your own of a true "all" statement (all of Group A are Group B) and a "some" statement (some of Group B are Group A) will help you to develop a mastery of this concept.

More examples:

| True: | All the people at my party speak Spanish. |
| Therefore, Valid: | Some people who speak Spanish are at my party. |

| True: | All Supreme Court justices are lawyers. |
| Therefore, Valid: | Some lawyers are Supreme Court justices. |

| True: | All U.S. Presidents were elected. |
| Therefore, Valid: | Some officials who were elected are U.S. Presidents. |

| True: | Every U.S. Border Patrol Agent works for the U.S. Government. |
| Therefore, Valid: | Some employees of the U.S. Government are U.S. Border Patrol Agents. |

| True: | Every U.S. Senator is a member of the U.S. Congress. |
| Therefore, Valid: | Some members of the U.S. Congress are U.S. Senators. |

Reasoning From "None" and "Not" Statements

Information that something is **NOT** true is useful information. For example, you may learn that one group of things is **NOT** part of another group of things. This is the same as saying that there is no overlap at all between the two groups of things. Here, you can draw conclusions about either group as it relates to the other since you can count on the fact that the two groups have no members in common. If you can say that no reptiles are warm-blooded, you can **also** say that no warm-blooded creatures are reptiles because you know that the first statement means that there is no overlap between the two groups. In the test, you will see phrases or terms such as "It is not the case that" or "Not all of" or words that begin with the prefix "non-." All of these are ways to say that a negative fact has been established.

Sometimes, our ordinary speech habits can cause us to jump to conclusions. Most people would not make a statement such as "Some of the pizza has no pepperoni" unless they are trying to suggest at the same time that some of the pizza **does** have pepperoni. By contrast, a detective might make a statement such as "some of the bloodstains were not human blood" simply because only part of the samples had come back from the laboratory. The detective is trying to suggest that <u>at least</u> some of the bloodstains were not human blood. The rest of the bloodstains might or might not be human blood.

As you work through the practice test, think about each negative phrase or term you find. Take care to assume only as much as is definitely indicated by the facts as given, and no more.

Reasoning About Parts of a Group

The term "some" refers to a part of a larger group. For example, in the statement "Some agents are taking specialized training," the term "some agents" refers to a portion of the group of all agents. You should note, however, that the fact that we know that "some agents are taking specialized training" implies nothing about the remaining portion of the set of agents: other agents may or may not be taking specialized training. Unless information is provided in the paragraph to the contrary, treat "some" as meaning "at least some."

Statements that refer to a portion of a set may contain other terms such as "most," "a few," or "almost all." Also, as discussed in the previous section, they can be negative, as in "Many agents are not fluent in French." From this statement you may be tempted to infer that there are at least a few agents who <u>are</u> fluent in French, but that would be jumping to a conclusion. From this statement alone, you do not know about the entire group of agents and whether or not they are fluent in French. In these cases, you should remember that the term refers only to a part of the group and that from this information on part of the group you cannot infer anything about the rest of the group. Unfortunately, neglecting this principle of sound reasoning can cause costly errors.

When you see a paragraph describing parts of a group, read the paragraph carefully to see if that description is based on knowledge of the entire group or only on knowledge of part of the group.

Reasoning About "If-Then" Statements

As was said before, there can be information about events or situations, and there can be information about individuals and groups. Previously, Section II discussed how to deal with information about groups. Next, Section II will discuss how to deal with information about the relationship between events or situations.

We are all familiar with the idea of a *chain of events* in which one thing leads to another thing, which in turn leads to a third thing, and so on. For example, "if a person is convicted of possession of a gram of marijuana in Aker County, that person is guilty of a misdemeanor, and persons found guilty of a misdemeanor in Aker County are fined by the court." It is easy to see that one can think backward and forward along this chain.

Thinking forward means that, when the first thing happens, the later events will follow. For example, if you learn that Bill is convicted of possession of a gram of marijuana in Aker County, you know that Bill is guilty of a misdemeanor. Furthermore, if you know that Bill is guilty of a misdemeanor in Aker County, you know that Bill will be fined by the court.

Thinking backward means that if later events do not occur, the earlier events did not occur. For example, if you know that Bill has never been fined by the court in Aker County, you know that he has not been found guilty of a misdemeanor there. Furthermore, by reasoning backward from the fact that Bill has not been found guilty of a misdemeanor in Aker County, you know that he has never been convicted of possession of a gram of marijuana there.

The wording we typically use to indicate this kind of linkage between events includes the simple "if-then" sentence in which the first event is in a statement tagged by "if" and the second event is in a statement tagged by "then." An example would be the sentence "if Chris gets assigned to the Bike Patrol, then the Bike Patrol will need additional equipment." We also use the same language to describe signs that such a linkage has already happened. An example of that structure would be the sentence "If there are tracks on the ground, then people passed through this area on foot."

There are other ways of wording this relationship, however. When a sentence starts with the word "whenever," it means that a linkage between two events is being described: "Whenever I hear that song, I think about the beach." The phrases "each time" or "every time" suggest the same thing: "Every time there is a power surge, my computer switches off."

It is important to realize that you cannot validly switch the order of the two statements in this type of sentence. If you do, your conclusion may be wrong and may lead to costly errors in real-life situations. For example, you learn that "If the jet engines are reversed (the first statement), the speed of the plane will decrease very rapidly (the second statement)." From this information, you cannot validly infer that "If the speed of the plane decreases very rapidly (the second statement), then the jet engines have been reversed (the first statement)". The following examples start with a true "if-then" sentence, followed by an invalid "if-then" sentence with the first and second statements reversed.

True:	If a person is a Border Patrol Agent, the person is an employee of the U.S. Government.
Therefore, Invalid:	If a person is an employee of the U.S. Government, the person is a Border Patrol Agent.
True:	If a criminal receives a pardon, the criminal will be released.
Therefore, Invalid:	If a criminal is released, the criminal has received a pardon.
True:	If a person is convicted of murder, that person is guilty of a felony.
Therefore, Invalid:	If a person is guilty of a felony, that person has been convicted of murder.
True:	If a person lives in Germany, the person lives in Europe.
Therefore, Invalid:	If a person lives in Europe, the person lives in Germany.
True:	If a car has no gas, the car will not run.
Therefore, Invalid:	If a car does not run, the car has no gas.

You can, however, validly reverse the order of these two statements when the statements are made opposite (that is, negated). For example, you learn that "If the jet engines are reversed (the first statement), the speed of the plane will decrease very rapidly (the second statement)." From this information, you can validly infer that "If the speed of the plane does not decrease very rapidly (the negation or opposite of the second statement), then the jet engines have not been reversed (the negation or opposite of the first statement)". The following examples start with a true "if-then" sentence, followed by a true (or valid) "if-then" sentence with the first and second statements made opposite (negated) and reversed in order.

True:	If a person is a Border Patrol Agent, the person is an employee of the U.S. Government.
Therefore, True:	If a person is not an employee of the U.S. Government, the person is not a Border Patrol Agent.
True:	If a criminal receives a pardon, the criminal will be released.
Therefore, True:	If a criminal is not released, the criminal has not received a pardon.
True:	If a person is convicted of murder, that person is guilty of a felony.
Therefore, True:	If a person is not guilty of a felony, that person has not been convicted of murder.
True:	If a person lives in Germany, the person lives in Europe.
Therefore, True:	If a person does not live in Europe, the person does not live in Germany.
True:	If a car has no gas, the car will not run.
Therefore, True:	If a car runs, the car has gas.

You cannot infer the opposite of the second statement from the opposite of the first statement. For example, you cannot validly infer that "If the jet engines are not reversed (the opposite of the first statement), then the speed of the plane does not decrease very rapidly (the opposite of the second statement)". The following examples start with a true "if-then" sentence followed by an invalid "if-then" sentence made of the opposite of the first and second statements.

True:	If a person is a Border Patrol Agent, the person is an employee of the U.S. Government.
Therefore, Invalid:	If a person is not a Border Patrol Agent, the person is not an employee of the U.S. Government.
True:	If a criminal receives a pardon, the criminal will be released.
Therefore, Invalid:	If a criminal does not receive a pardon, the criminal will not be released.
True:	If a person is convicted of murder, that person is guilty of a felony.
Therefore, Invalid:	If a person is not convicted of murder, that person is not guilty of a felony.
True:	If a person lives in Germany, the person lives in Europe.
Therefore, Invalid:	If a person does not live in Germany, the person does not live in Europe.
True:	If a car has no gas, the car will not run.
Therefore, Invalid:	If a car has gas, the car will run.

A Few Final Cautions About Wording

There are test preparation classes that train people to take tests. In some of these courses, students are advised against choosing any answer in a reasoning test if it starts with the word "all" or the word "none." This is supposed to be useful advice because it is believed that most correct answers strike a balance between extremes and usually do not cover subjects that can be summarized in sentences beginning with "all" or "none." If you have heard this advice before, you should ignore it for this test. "All" statements and "none" statements occur in real-life situations and, consequently, you will be asked to work with them in this test in the reading paragraphs as well as in both correct and incorrect responses.

In general, you should pay attention to any words that provide information on groups or on linked events. This includes a wide range of negative words (such as "seldom" or "never" or "illegal" or "prohibited") and negative prefixes (such as "non-" "un-" or "dis-"). It also includes positive words (such as "all" or "some" or "most" or "always"). You should also watch for connectors such as "whenever" or "unless" or "except," since these words sometimes contain key information about relations among the facts given in the paragraph.

English is a language that ordinarily uses single negatives. The word "not," by itself, does the job of making a formal English sentence into its opposite: "That bird is NOT an eagle." On this test, if you read a sentence such as "The cord is not wound," it means the cord is still unwound. When an English sentence has two negatives, the sentence has a positive meaning. For example, a sentence that reads "This application is NOT unworthy" means that the application IS worthy. The sentence "The bell did ring" could be stated "It is NOT the case that the bell did NOT ring."

Finally, it is extremely important to pay close attention to the use of the word "ONLY." A sentence such as "The door will open IF AND ONLY IF both keys are used" is a very strong statement that means that there is just one way to open the door—with both keys. If the sentence just said, "The door will open if the key is used," there may be several other ways to open the door. But that is not the case when the expression "if and only if" is used.

Remember These Tips When Taking the Logical Reasoning Test

1. In questions with positive lead statements, always choose the only conclusion that can <u>definitely</u> be drawn from the information given in the paragraph.

2. Remember NOT to use any outside factual information to reach your conclusion.

3. Read the lead-in sentence and the paragraph very carefully. Also, read all the answer choices before you mark the one you think is correct.

4. Pay special attention whenever the question uses words such as "all," "some," or "none." Other terms such as "unless" or "except" or "only" are also important. These words help to define the facts from which you must draw conclusions.

5. Also pay special attention whenever you see a negative prefix such as "non-" or a negative verb such as "<u>dis</u>connect" or "<u>un</u>fasten." These may be crucial to understanding the basic facts in the paragraph.

6. Ignore any advice you may have received in the past about avoiding an answer that contains the word "all" or the word "none." These may be signs of an incorrect response in some tests, but not in this test. You will find these words in both right and wrong response options.

7. Take the sample test and study the explanation for each of the questions very carefully. This will help you fine-tune your reasoning on the actual test.

LOGICAL REASONING PRACTICE TEST

*In questions 1 through 8, some questions will ask you to select the only answer that can be validly concluded from the paragraph. These questions include a paragraph followed by five response options. Preceding the five response options will be the phrase "From the information given above, it can be validly concluded that." In other questions you may be asked to select the only answer that **cannot** be validly concluded from the paragraph. These questions include a paragraph followed by five response options. Preceding the five response options will be the phrase "From the information given above, it **CANNOT** be validly concluded that."*

*You must use **only** the information provided in the paragraph, without using any outside information whatsoever.*

It is suggested that you take not more than 20 minutes to complete questions 1 through 8. The questions on this practice test will not be on the real test, but the real questions will be similar in form and difficulty to these. The explanations for the correct and incorrect responses are found after the sample questions.

1. Often, crimes are characterized as either *malum in se*—inherently evil—or *malum prohibitum*—criminal because they are declared as offenses by a legislature. Murder is an example of the former. Failing to file a tax return illustrates the latter. Some jurisdictions no longer distinguish between crimes *malum in se* and *malum prohibitum*, although many still do.

    From the information given above, it can be validly concluded that

    A) many jurisdictions no longer distinguish between crimes *malum in se* and *malum prohibitum*
    B) some jurisdictions still distinguish between crimes *malum in se* and *malum prohibitum*
    C) some crimes characterized as *malum in se* are not inherently evil
    D) some crimes characterized as *malum prohibitum* are not declared by a legislature to be an offense
    E) sometimes failing to file a tax return is characterized as *malum in se*

2. A trucking company can act as a *common carrier*—for hire to the general public at published rates. As a common carrier, it is liable for any cargo damage, unless the company can show that it was not negligent. If the company can demonstrate that it was not negligent, then it is not liable for cargo damage. In contrast, a *contract carrier* (a trucking company hired by a shipper under a specific contract) is only responsible for cargo damage as spelled out in the contract. A Claus Inc. tractor-trailer, acting under common carrier authority, was in a 5-vehicle accident that damaged its cargo. A Nichols Inc. tractor-trailer, acting under contract carrier authority, was involved in the same accident, and its cargo was also damaged.

    From the information given above, it can be validly concluded that, in reference to the accident,

    A) if Claus Inc. is liable, then it can show that it was not negligent
    B) if Claus Inc. cannot show that it was not negligent, then it is not liable
    C) if Claus Inc. can show that it was not negligent, then it is not liable
    D) if Nichols Inc. is liable, then it cannot show that it is negligent
    E) if Nichols Inc. can show that it is not negligent, then it is not liable

3. A rapidly changing technical environment in government is promoting greater reliance on electronic mail (e-mail) systems. As this usage grows, there are increasing chances of conflict between the users' expectations of privacy and public access rights. In some investigations, access to <u>all</u> e-mail, including those messages stored in archival files and messages outside the scope of the investigation, has been sought and granted. In spite of this, some people send messages through e-mail that would never be said face-to-face or written formally.

*From the information given above, it **CANNOT** be validly concluded that*

A) some e-mail messages that have been requested as part of investigations have contained messages that would never be said face-to-face
B) some messages that people would never say face-to-face are sent in e-mail messages
C) some e-mail messages have been requested as part of investigations
D) e-mail messages have not been exempted from investigations
E) some e-mail messages contain information that would be omitted from formal writing

4. Phyllis T. is a former Federal employee who was entitled to benefits under the Federal Employee Compensation Act because of a job-related, disabling injury. When an eligible Federal employee has such an injury, the benefit is determined by this test: If the beneficiary is married or has dependents, benefits are 3/4 of the person's salary at the time of the injury; otherwise, benefits are set at 2/3 of the salary. Phyllis T.'s benefits were 2/3 of her salary when she was injured.

From the information given above, it can be validly concluded that, when Phyllis T. was injured, she

A) was married but without dependents
B) was not married and had no dependents
C) was not married but had dependents
D) was married and had dependents
E) had never been married

5. Some 480,000 immigrants were living in a certain country in 1999. Although most of these immigrants were not employed in professional occupations, many of them were. For instance, many of them were engineers and many of them were nurses. Very few of these immigrants were librarians, another professional occupation.

From the information given above, it can be validly concluded that, in 1999, in the country described above,

A) most immigrants were either engineers or nurses
B) it is not the case that some of the nurses were immigrants
C) none of the engineers were immigrants
D) most of those not employed in professional occupations were immigrants
E) some of the engineers were immigrants

6. Police officers were led to believe that many weapons sold at a certain gun store were sold illegally. Upon investigating the lead, the officers learned that all of the weapons sold by the store that were made by Precision Arms were sold legally. Also, none of the illegally sold weapons were .45 caliber.

    From the information given above, it can be validly concluded that, concerning the weapons sold at the store,

    A) all of the .45 caliber weapons were made by Precision Arms
    B) none of the .45 caliber weapons were made by Precision Arms
    C) some of the weapons made by Precision Arms were .45 caliber weapons
    D) all of the .45 caliber weapons were sold legally
    E) some of the weapons made by Precision Arms were sold illegally

7. Impressions made by the ridges on the ends of the fingers and thumbs are useful means of identification, since no two persons have the same pattern of ridges. If finger patterns from fingerprints are not decipherable, then they cannot be classified by general shape and contour or by pattern type. If they cannot be classified by these characteristics, then it is impossible to identify the person to whom the fingerprints belong.

    *From the information given above, it **CANNOT** be validly concluded that*

    A) if it is possible to identify the person to whom fingerprints belong, then the fingerprints are decipherable
    B) if finger patterns from fingerprints are not decipherable, then it is impossible to identify the person to whom the fingerprints belong
    C) if fingerprints are decipherable, then it is impossible to identify the person to whom they belong
    D) if fingerprints can be classified by general shape and contour or by pattern type, then they are decipherable
    E) if it is possible to identify the person to whom fingerprints belong, then the fingerprints can be classified by general shape and contour or pattern type

8. Explosives are substances or devices capable of producing a volume of rapidly expanding gases that exert a sudden pressure on their surroundings. Chemical explosives are the most commonly used, although there are mechanical and nuclear explosives. All mechanical explosives are devices in which a physical reaction is produced, such as that caused by overloading a container with compressed air. While nuclear explosives are by far the most powerful, all nuclear explosives have been restricted to military weapons.

    From the information given above, it can be validly concluded that

    A) all explosives that have been restricted to military weapons are nuclear explosives
    B) no mechanical explosives are devices in which a physical reaction is produced, such as that caused by overloading a container with compressed air
    C) some nuclear explosives have not been restricted to military weapons
    D) all mechanical explosives have been restricted to military weapons
    E) some devices in which a physical reaction is produced, such as that caused by overloading a container with compressed air, are mechanical explosives

ANALYSIS OF LOGICAL REASONING PRACTICE TEST QUESTIONS

1. **Correct Answer: B)** some jurisdictions still distinguish between crimes *malum in se* and *malum prohibitum*.

This question is concerned with classification of crimes into sets—that is, with the classification of crimes as either *malum in se* or *malum prohibitum*. The last phrase in the last sentence tells us that many jurisdictions make the distinction between these two categories of crimes. Response B follows from that sentence, because if many jurisdictions make the distinction, some jurisdictions make the distinction. From the fact that many jurisdictions make the distinction, it cannot be inferred that many do <u>not</u> make the distinction. Therefore, Response A is incorrect.

Responses C, D, and E are based on erroneous definitions of the two classes of crimes. The paragraph tells us that all crimes characterized as *malum in se* are inherently evil. Response C is false because it cannot be the case that SOME crimes characterized as *malum in se* are NOT inherently evil. The paragraph also tells us that all crimes characterized as *malum prohibitum* are declared as offenses by a legislature. Response D is false because it cannot be the case that SOME crimes characterized as *malum prohibitum* are NOT declared by a legislature to be an offense. In the paragraph, we are told that filing a tax return late is *malum prohibitum*, rather than *malum in se*. Response E is incorrect because it cannot be the case that failing to file a tax return is *malum in se*.

2. **Correct Answer: C)** If Claus Inc. can show that it was not negligent, then it is not liable.

The second sentence states the liability rule for common carriers: all common carriers are liable for cargo damage unless they can show that they are not negligent; if they can show that they are not negligent, then they are not liable for cargo damage. Claus Inc. is a common carrier, and accordingly this rule applies to it. From this rule it follows that if Claus Inc. can show it was not negligent, then it is not liable, Response C. Response A contradicts this rule by claiming that when Claus Inc. is liable it can show that it was not negligent. Response B contradicts this rule by claiming that Claus Inc. is not liable even when it cannot show that it is not negligent. Responses D and E concern Nichols Inc., a contract carrier. However, the terms of the Nichols Inc. contract were not disclosed in the paragraph, so neither response is supported.

3. **Correct Answer: A)** some e-mail messages that have been requested as part of investigations have contained messages that would never be said face-to-face.

This is an example of a test question with a negative lead-in statement. It asks for the conclusion that is **NOT** supported by the paragraph. That means that four of the statements are valid conclusions from the paragraph while one is not. Response B (some messages that people would never say face-to-face are sent in e-mail messages) is a valid conclusion because it restates a fact given in the last sentence of the paragraph. Response E (some e-mail messages contain information that would be omitted from formal writing) is valid because it restates the other fact in the last sentence of the paragraph.

The next-to-last sentence in the paragraph is the source of both response C (some e-mail messages have been requested as part of investigations) and response D (e-mail messages have not been exempted from investigations). Both of these choices restate information in that sentence, based on the fact that access to e-mail messages was sought and granted. This leaves only the first option, response A (Some e-mail messages that have been requested as part of investigations have contained messages that would never be said face-to-face). This is the only choice that does **NOT** represent a valid conclusion, because even though we know from the paragraph that there is a group of e-mail messages that are requested in investigations and also that there is a group of messages that contain information that people would not say face-to-face, there is nothing that says that these groups overlap. We simply do not know.

4. Correct Answer: B) Phyllis T. was not married and had no dependents.

This question concerns an either/or situation. The paragraph states that benefits under the Federal Employees Compensation Act are awarded at one level (3/4 of salary) if a beneficiary is married or has dependents when injured and at another level (2/3 of salary) if this is not true.

Phyllis T. is eligible for benefits under the Act. The paragraph states that Phyllis T.'s benefit level was 2/3 of her salary. Given this benefit level, it is clear that Phyllis T. did not meet either of the conditions for the 3/4 level. Therefore, responses A, C, and D cannot be correct (A states that she was married, C states that she had dependents, and D states that she both was married and had dependents). Response E goes beyond the facts given because prior marriages are not listed as a factor relating to this benefit. The one correct conclusion is that Phyllis T. did not meet either requirement to qualify for the higher benefit level (3/4 of salary), so response B is the correct answer to the question.

5. Correct Answer: E) some of the engineers were immigrants

Response E is correct because it restates the third sentence in terms of the overlap between immigrants and engineers in the country described in the paragraph. Response A says that most immigrants are engineers or nurses, which are professional occupations. However, the second sentence says that most immigrants are not employed in professional occupations, so Response A is false. Response B is false because it denies that there is any overlap between immigrants and nurses, even though this overlap is clear from the third sentence of the paragraph. Response C is false because it denies the overlap between immigrants and engineers. Because the paragraph does not give complete information about the non-professionals (immigrant and non-immigrant) in the country described in the paragraph, Response D is invalid.

6. Correct Answer: D) all of the .45 caliber weapons were sold legally

The second and last sentences are the two main premises in the paragraph. These two sentences give information about three categories of weapons: weapons made by Precision Arms, weapons sold legally, and .45 caliber weapons.

The last sentence states that none of the illegally sold weapons were .45 caliber. This means that none of the .45 caliber weapons were sold illegally. Notice that this new statement is a double negative. In affirmative form the statement means that all of the .45 caliber weapons were sold legally, Choice D.

The information that all of the .45 caliber weapons were sold legally (last sentence), combined with the information that all of the weapons made by Precision Arms were sold legally (second sentence), allows us to draw no valid conclusions about the relationship between the .45 caliber weapons and the weapons made by Precision Arms. There is insufficient information about the entire group of weapons sold legally to know whether the group of .45 caliber weapons and the group of weapons made by Precision Arms overlapped entirely (Choice A), partially (Choice C), or not at all (Choice B).

Choice E contradicts the second sentence and is, therefore, invalid.

7. **Correct Answer: C)** if fingerprints are decipherable, then it is impossible to identify the
    person to whom they belong

This question asks for the response option that **cannot** be validly concluded from the information in the paragraph. The only response option that cannot be validly concluded is Response C, so the correct answer to question 7 is Response C. Response C is invalid because the paragraph does not provide enough information to conclude whether or not it would be possible to identify the person to whom the fingerprints belong from the mere fact that the fingerprints are decipherable.

Response A refers to a condition where it is possible to identify the person to whom fingerprints belong. Based on the final sentence in the paragraph, this condition of fingerprints means that the fingerprints could be classified by general shape and contour or by pattern type. Based on the second sentence, the ability to classify the fingerprints means that the fingerprints are decipherable.

Since Response B refers to a condition in which finger patterns from fingerprints are not decipherable, we know from the second sentence that, in that circumstance, they cannot be classified by general shape and contour or by pattern type. From the final sentence in the paragraph, we can infer that since they cannot be classified by these characteristics, then it is impossible to identify the person to whom the fingerprints belong.

According to the second sentence, fingerprints cannot be classified by general shape and contour or by pattern type when they are not decipherable. Therefore, if fingerprints can be classified by general shape and contour or by pattern type, then the fingerprints must be decipherable, Response D. According to the third sentence, it is impossible to identify the owner of a set of fingerprints when the fingerprints cannot be classified by general shape and contour or by pattern type. Therefore, if it is possible to identify the person to whom fingerprints belong, then the fingerprints must be able to be classified by general shape and contour or pattern type, Response E. Notice that Responses D and E are valid based on the same type of reasoning. The first and second statements of the second sentence were made opposite and reversed in Response D, and the first and second statements of the final sentence were made opposite and reversed in Response E.

8. Correct Answer: E) some devices in which a physical reaction is produced, such as that caused by overloading a container with compressed air, are mechanical explosives

The correct answer is E. The third sentence states the overlap between all mechanical explosives and devices in which a physical reaction is produced, such as that caused by overloading a container with compressed air. From this, we can safely conclude that some devices in which a physical reaction is produced, such as that caused by overloading a container with compressed air, are mechanical explosives.

Response A is incorrect because the paragraph does not provide sufficient information to validly conclude that all explosives which have been restricted to military weapons are nuclear weapons. It may be that some types of explosives other than nuclear weapons also have been restricted to military weapons.

Responses B and C are incorrect because they contradict the paragraph. Response B contradicts the third sentence, and Response C contradicts the last sentence.

Response D is incorrect because the paragraph provides no information about whether or not mechanical explosives are restricted to military weapons.

Section III. Sample Questions for the Spanish Language Proficiency Test

INTRODUCTION

Purpose of this Section

The purpose of this Section is to provide you with information about the Spanish Language Proficiency Test. All Border Patrol Agents are required to know the Spanish language. Accordingly, all applicants for the position of Border Patrol Agent are required to take either the Spanish Language Proficiency Test or the ALT. Applicants who already know Spanish should take the Spanish Language Proficiency Test; all other applicants should take the ALT. The sample questions in this section will make you very familiar with both the type and the difficulty level of the questions on the Spanish Language Proficiency Test, thus giving you a guide to judge whether you should take the Spanish Language Proficiency Test or the ALT.

These sample questions and explanations are not intended to teach you enough Spanish to pass the Spanish Language Proficiency Test. The purpose of these questions and explanations is to make you familiar with the types of questions on the Spanish Language Proficiency Test.

Organization of this Section

The Spanish Language Proficiency Test is divided into two parts. The first part consists entirely of *vocabulary* questions; the second part is divided into three sections, each section dealing with a different type of *grammar* question. The following pages contain four examples of each type of question included in the Spanish Language Proficiency Test.

Sample Questions for the Spanish Language Proficiency Test

<u>PART I</u>

Read the sentence and then choose the most appropriate synonym for the underlined word.

1. Es muy *complicado* pilotar mi avión.

    A) fácil
    B) difícil
    C) divertido
    D) compilado
    E) comparado

The word *complicado* means <u>complicated</u>. In the context of the sentence, it refers to something that is hard to do. Hence, response B, *difícil* ("difficult"), is the best synonym. Response A, *fácil* ("easy"), is opposite in meaning to *complicado*. Response C, *divertido,* has the same beginning syllable ("di-") as the correct answer, but its meaning ("amusing") is completely different. The basic meanings of responses D and E ("compiled" and "compared," respectively) are completely different from the meaning of *complicado,* although both *compilado* and *comparado* are phonetically similar to it.

2. Es fácil *comprender* lo que el agente está diciendo.

    A) responder
    B) comprobar
    C) entender
    D) pretender
    E) desentender

The word *comprender* means to understand something after watching, listening to, or reading it. Hence, response C, *entender* ("to understand"), is the best synonym. Response E, *desentender*, is the exact opposite of the correct answer; in fact, it is *entender*, but with a negative prefix added to it, thus giving it the meaning of "to misunderstand." Responses A, B, and D ("to respond," "to verify," and "to pretend") are completely unrelated to the meaning of *comprender.*

3. Hay que <u>esclarecer</u> todo el proceso.

    A) encontrar
    B) concentrar
    C) aclarar
    D) empeorar
    E) aplastar

The word *esclarecer* means <u>to clarify</u>. Hence, response C, *aclarar* ("to clarify"), is the best synonym. Responses A, B, D, and E ("to find," "to concentrate," "to worsen," and "to crush") are completely unrelated to the meaning of *esclarecer*.

4. Hemos otorgado <u>concesiones</u> especiales a los países en vías de desarrollo.

    A) privilegios
    B) determinaciones
    C) estipendios
    D) cortesías
    E) ofrendas

The word *concesiones* means <u>concessions</u>, rights or privileges that have been granted. Hence, response A, *privilegios* ("privileges") is the best synonym. Responses B, C, D, and E ("determinations," "stipends," "courtesies," and "offerings") are completely unrelated to the meaning of *concesiones*.

PART II

Section I

Read each sentence carefully. Select the appropriate word or phrase to fill each blank space.

1. Me gusta entrar _____ la puerta que está _____ de la oficina.

    A) a, sobre
    B) en, desde
    C) con, bajo
    D) en, al lado
    E) por, detrás

The correct answer is response E, *por, detrás*. Responses A, B, C, and D all use incorrect prepositions.

2. La agente me _____ la correspondencia cuando yo no _____ en casa.

    A) traido, estoy
    B) traer, estuviera
    C) trajo, estaba
    D) traerá, habré estado
    E) habrá traido, estar

The correct answer is response C, *trajo, estaba,* because both verbs represent the correct past tense in the indicative mood (preterite indefinite <u>trajo</u> and preterite imperfect <u>estaba</u>). In responses A, B, D, and E, the wrong forms of the verb have been used.

3. Los oficiales _____ usan la sala de reuniones para discutir asuntos _____.

    A) sumariamente / difícil
    B) frecuentemente / variadas
    C) normalmente / diversos
    D) rara vez / personal
    E) ocasionalmente / unilateral

Choice C is the correct answer. The adverb *normalmente* ("normally") correctly modifies the verb *usan* ("[they] use"), and the plural, masculine adjective *diversos* ("diverse") agrees in gender and number with the noun it modifies ("asuntos"). In responses A, D, and E, there is no agreement in number between adjective and noun. In response B, there is no agreement in gender between adjective and noun.

4. _____ a los detenidos y _____ al tanto de los resultados.

    A) Visita / pónlos
    B) Visite / ponerlos
    C) Visitaré / ponga
    D) Habré visitado / pondré
    E) Visitando / había puesto

Response A is the correct answer. The two imperative verb forms [tú] *visita* and [tú] *pónlos* are the correct choices. In responses B, C, D, and E, there is no agreement between the two main verbs.

Section II

Read each sentence carefully. Select the one sentence that is correct.

1. A) Todos los agentes coincidieron del sospechoso cuando entrarían por la puerta.
    B) El sospechoso que entró fue señalado en la puerta con los agentes coincidiendo.
    C) Todos los agentes señalaron al mismo sospechoso cuando entró por la puerta.
    D) Todos los agentes coincidió en señalar al sospechoso cuando entrarán por la puerta.

The correct answer to this item is response C because it has the proper sentence structure (subject, verb, direct object) and contains no errors. Responses A, B, and D contain various errors, including incorrect prepositions, illogical structures, or incorrect verb forms; hence, none of them can be the correct answer.

2. A) La inmigración ilegal y el contrabando suponen un gran problema para muchos países.
    B) La inmigración ilegal y el contrabando supongo un problema grande para muchos países.
    C) Muchos países con gran problemas suponían la inmigración ilegal y el contrabando.
    D) La inmigración ilegales y el contrabando suponen un gran problema para muchos países.

The correct answer to this item is response A because it has the proper sentence structure (subject, verb, direct object, indirect object) and contains no errors. Responses B, C, and D contain various errors, including incorrect terms, illogical structures, or incorrect verb forms; hence, none of these responses can be the correct answer.

3. A) Como el agente sabía que andando es bueno para la salud, andaría unos veinte minutos antes de iniciar el entrenamiento oficial.
    B) Como el agente sabía que andar es bueno para la salud, anduvo unos veinte minutos antes de iniciar el entrenamiento oficial.
    C) Andaría unos veinte minutos como andar es bueno sabía el agente antes de iniciar el entrenamiento oficial.
    D) Que andar es bueno para la salud unos veinte minutos antes de había iniciado el entrenamiento oficial el agente sabía que andaría.

The correct answer to this item is response B because it has the proper sentence structure (subject, verb, direct object) and contains no errors. Responses A, C, and D contain various errors, including incorrect terms, misplaced clauses, or disagreement of verb tenses; hence, none of these responses can be the correct answer.

4. A) Aunque hay países donde existen varias agrupaciones de derechos humanos que se preocupan por velar sobre las garantías individuales y que resultan muy efectivas en ciertas sociedades en que su esfera de influencia es muy limitada o casi nula.
    B) Existen varias agrupaciones internacionales de derechos humanos que se preocupan por velar sobre las garantías individuales y que resultan muy efectivas en ciertas sociedades, aunque hay países en que su esfera de influencia es muy limitada o casi nula.
    C) Existen de derechos humanos varias agrupaciones internacionales que se preocupan por velar sobre las garantías individuales, aunque hay países en que su esfera de influencia que resultan muy efectivas en ciertas sociedades es muy limitada o casi nula.
    D) Hay países en que existen varias agrupaciones internacionales de derechos humanos y que resultan muy efectivas en ciertas sociedades aunque que se preocupan por velar sobre las garantías individuales en que su esfera de influencia es muy limitada o casi nula.

The correct answer to this item is response B because it has the proper sentence structure (subject, verb, direct object, indirect object) and contains no errors. Responses A, C, and D contain misplaced clauses; hence, none of these responses can be the correct answer.

Section III

Read each sentence carefully. Select the correct word or phrase to replace the underlined portions of the sentence. In those cases in which the sentence needs no correction, select alternative (E).

1. Los agentes detectaron el contrabando antes de <u>abrir</u> la maleta.

    A) abriendo
    B) abrirá
    C) abriremos
    D) abrió
    E) No es necesario hacer ninguna corrección.

The correct answer to this item is response E because the infinitive form of the verb, *abrir*, must be used after the preposition *de*. Incorrect forms of the verb have been used in the other responses; namely, response A (gerund), response B (future imperfect), response C (future imperfect), and response D (preterite indefinite).

2. Es necesario tener <u>todo las</u> documentos de identificación en regla.

    A) todos las
    B) todo el
    C) todas las
    D) todos los
    E) No es necesario hacer ninguna corrección.

The correct answer is response D because *todos los* is plural in number and masculine in gender, and is thus in agreement with *documentos*. Responses A, B, and C have either the wrong gender or the wrong number.

3. Los manuales <u>hemos abarcado</u> un sinnúmero de posibilidades y <u>hemos abreviado</u> el tiempo que se necesita para completar los trámites.

    A) abarcando / abreviando
    B) abarcados / abreviados
    C) abarcó / abrevió
    D) abarcan / abrevian
    E) No es necesario hacer ninguna corrección.

Response D is the correct answer because the two verbs in the third person plural [*abarcan* ("cover") and *abrevian* ("shorten")] agree with the masculine plural subject *manuales* ("manuals").

Responses A and B use incorrect verb forms (gerund and participle). In responses C and E, there is no agreement between verbs and subject.

4. Los que <u>abastecen</u> las cocinas de las unidades de rescate <u>anoche</u> trajeron magníficas provisiones.

    A) habían abastecido / lentamente
    B) abasteciendo / no
    C) abastecieran / mañana
    D) abastezco / arriba
    E) No es necesario hacer ninguna corrección.

Response E is the correct answer because the present indicative verb *abastecen* ("[they] supply") agrees with the preterite indefinite *trajeron* ("[they] brought") after the correctly selected adverb *anoche* ("last night"). In response A, the adverb of manner *lentamente* ("slowly") is incorrect. Responses B and C use the wrong verb form. Response D does not have agreement in number between subject and verb.

Section IV: Preparing for the Artificial Language Test

INTRODUCTION

Purpose of this Section

The purpose of this section is to help you to prepare for the Artificial Language Test (ALT). This test is intended to assess an applicant's ability to learn Spanish. The test is based on an artificial language, the rules of which are based on some of the grammatical structures of Spanish. Because all Border Patrol Agents are required to know the Spanish language, it is important to assess language-learning abilities in all applicants to the Border Patrol Agent occupation who do not already know Spanish. A validation study conducted by the U.S. Office of Personnel Management and an attrition study conducted at the Border Patrol Academy demonstrated that the ALT is an extremely effective predictor of success in learning Spanish at the Academy. Accordingly, you are encouraged to study this manual with special care and attention.

This section is designed to allow every opportunity for you to study the grammatical rules of the Artificial Language prior to taking the ALT. In this way, you can spend concentrated time in learning to use grammatical rules that you will need to apply not only in the test, but also in the process of learning Spanish, if you are selected for a Border Patrol Agent (Trainee) position.

Organization of this Section

Section IV contains several parts: vocabulary lists (or dictionary) for the Artificial Language, a set of grammatical rules, a glossary of grammatical terms (for applicants who do not remember the meaning of some of these terms), a practice test, which is similar in format and length to the actual test, and, lastly, a clear and concise explanation of why each response in the test is right or wrong. This last part should greatly assist you in learning how to apply each of the rules. The parts of this section are organized in the following sequence.

First: The Vocabulary Lists

The lists of words need not be memorized because during the actual test they will be available to you for constant consultation.

Second: The Glossary of Grammatical Rules for the Artificial Language

These rules are the essence of the Artificial Language because they are the essence of its connection to the structures of the Spanish language. There is no need to memorize the rules because they will be available to you during the test. Also, you should note that some of the rules will be different in the actual test. For example, if the feminine form of a noun takes the suffix nef in the rules presented in this manual, in the actual test the feminine form of a noun may take a different ending.

Third: Glossary of Grammatical Terms

This glossary will provide a refresher mini-course in grammatical terms (such as "verb," "noun," "adjective," and "adverb") for applicants who have forgotten the meaning of these terms. The glossary will also be available for consultation during the actual test. In this section, however, the meaning of the terms will be discussed in greater depth, and it is therefore advisable for you to study the discussion here with special attention and concentration.

Fourth: The Practice Test

The practice test is similar, but not exactly the same, in length and format, and in its application of the grammatical rules to the actual test.

The practice test questions contain tasks that require a correct translation from English to the Artificial Language and that require the application of grammatical rules to Artificial Language sentences. In some cases, these tasks involve an entire sentence, while in others they involve only part of a sentence.

While taking the practice test, you should refer to all the materials described above, that is, to the vocabulary lists, the grammatical rules for the Artificial Language, and the glossary of grammatical terms. During the actual test, you will be able to refer to these sources at all times. When taking the actual test, you will be given two booklets: One (called the "Supplemental Booklet") will contain the reference materials (the vocabulary lists, the grammatical rules, and the glossary of grammatical terms), while the other will contain the test questions. You will have access to the "Supplemental Booklet" at all times while taking the test, and you will be able to consult the reference materials in the Supplemental Booklet while answering the test questions. Therefore, it would be advisable for you to practice using the reference materials while taking the practice test.

Fifth: The Rationale for Each Response

The last part of this section contains a clear and concise explanation of why each response choice in the test is right or wrong. Since the test is a multiple-choice test, each response choice must be evaluated separately. Consequently, it is important for you to know which rule is pertinent to each response choice. As will be clear from the study of the explanations, some response choices (those that are correct) conform to the appropriate rules, while the majority of response choices (those that are incorrect) violate one or more of the rules.

It is very advisable for you to analyze each and every one of the explanations after taking the practice test. If you find that many of your answers to the test questions are incorrect, it would be a good idea for you to retake the practice test after (1) studying the rationale for each response choice, and (2) studying the grammatical rules once again, with more attention to detail.

THE VOCABULARY LISTS

The words on the following lists are the same; they are merely arranged differently, as they would be in a bilingual dictionary. In the first list, you can look up words in English to find their equivalent word in the Artificial Language. In the second list, you can look up words in the Artificial Language to find their equivalent word in English. During the actual test, you will have the vocabulary lists with you for consultation at all times. Nonetheless, you should note that the words given below are not the same as those given in the actual test. Therefore, it is best not to try to memorize them before taking the actual test.

Word List Arranged Alphabetically by the English Word

English	Artificial Language	English	Artificial Language
a, an	bex	skillful	janle
alien	huslek	that	velle
and	loa	the	wir
boy	ekaplek	this	volle
country	failek	to be	synker
difficult	glasle	to border	regker
enemy	avelek	to cross	chonker
friend	kometlek	to drive	arker
from	mor	to escape	pirker
government	almanlek	to guard	bonker
he, him	yev	to have	tulker
jeep	daqlek	to identify	kalenker
legal	colle	to injure	liaker
loyal	inle	to inspect	zelker
man	kaplek	to shoot	degker
of	quea	to spy	tatker
paper	trenedlek	to station	lexker
river	browlek	to work	frigker

Word List Arranged Alphabetically by the Artificial Language Word

Artificial Language	English	Artificial Language	English
almanlek	government	kaplek	man
arker	to drive	kometlek	friend
avelek	enemy	lexker	to station
bex	a, an	liaker	to injure
bonker	to guard	loa	and
browlek	river	mor	from
chonker	to cross	pirker	to escape
colle	legal	quea	of
daqlek	jeep	regker	to border
degker	to shoot	synker	to be
ekaplek	boy	tatker	to spy
failek	country	trenedlek	paper
frigker	to work	tulker	to have
glasle	difficult	velle	that
huslek	alien	volle	this
inle	loyal	wir	the
janle	skillful	yev	he, him
kalenker	to identify	zelker	to inspect

GRAMMATICAL RULES FOR THE ARTIFICIAL LANGUAGE

The grammatical rules given here are similar, but not identical, to those used in the ALT. Some of the suffixes (word endings) and prefixes (additions to the beginning of a word) used in the actual test differ from those used in the practice test.

During the actual test, you will have access to the rules at all times. Consequently, it is important that you understand these rules, but it is not necessary that you memorize them. In fact, memorizing them will hinder rather than help you, since there are differences between the rules in the version of the Artificial Language that appears here and the one that appears in the actual test.

You should note that the next part of this section contains a glossary of grammatical terms to assist you if you are not thoroughly familiar with the meaning of these grammatical terms.

Rule 1: To form the feminine singular of a noun, a pronoun, an adjective, or an article, add the suffix nef to the masculine singular form. Only nouns, pronouns, adjectives, and articles take feminine endings in the Artificial Language. When gender is not specified, the masculine form is used.

   Example: If a male eagle is a verlek, then a female eagle is a verleknef.
           If an ambitious man is a tosle man, an ambitious woman is a toslenef woman.

Rule 2: To form the plural of nouns, pronouns, adjectives, and articles, add the suffix oz to the correct singular form.

   Example: If one male eagle is a verlek, several male eagles are verlekoz.
           If an ambitious woman is a toslenef woman, several ambitious women are
           toslenefoz women.

Rule 3: Adjectives modifying nouns and pronouns with feminine and/or plural endings must have endings that agree with the words they modify. In addition, an article (a/an and the) preceding a noun must also agree with the noun in gender and number.

   Example: If an active male eagle is a sojle verlek, an active female eagle is a sojlenef
           verleknef and several active female eagles are sojlenefoz verleknefoz.
           If this male eagle is volle verlek, these female eagles are vollenefoz verleknefoz.
           If the male eagle is wir verlek, the female eagle is wirnef verleknef and the female
           eagles are wirnefoz verleknefoz.
           If a male eagle is bex verlek, several male eagles are bexoz verlekoz.

Rule 4: The stem of a verb is obtained by omitting the suffix ker from the infinitive form of the verb.

   Example: The stem of the verb tirker is tir.

Rule 5: All subjects and their verbs must agree in number; that is, singular subjects require singular verbs and plural subjects require plural verbs. (See Rules 6 and 7.)

Rule 6: To form the present tense of a verb, add the suffix em to the stem for the singular or the suffix im to the stem for the plural.

    Example: If to bark is nalker then nalem is the present tense for the singular (the dog barks) and nalim is the present tense for the plural (the dogs bark).

Rule 7: To form the past tense of a verb, first add the suffix zot to the stem, and then add the suffix em if the verb is singular or the suffix im if it is plural.

    Example: If to bark is nalker, then nalzotem is the past tense for the singular (the dog barked) and nalzotim is the past tense for the plural (the dogs barked).

Rule 8: To form the past participle of a verb, add to the stem of the verb the suffix to. It can be used to form compound tenses with the verb to have, as a predicate with the verb to be, or as an adjective. In the last two cases, it takes masculine, feminine, singular and plural forms in agreement with the noun to which it refers.

    An example of use in a compound tense with the verb to have:
        If to bark is nalker and to have is tulker, then tulem nalto is the *present perfect* for the singular (the dog has barked) and tulim nalto is the *present perfect* for the plural (the dogs have barked). Similarly, tulzotem nalto is the *past perfect* for the singular (the dog had barked) and tulzotim nalto is the *past perfect* for the plural (the dogs had barked).
    An example of use as a predicate with the verb to be:
        If to adopt is rapker and to be is synker, then a boy was adopted is a ekaplek synzotem rapto and many girls were adopted is ekapleknefoz synzotim raptonefoz.
    An example of use as an adjective:
        If to delight is kasker then a delighted boy is a kasto ekaplek and many delighted girls are kastonefoz ekapleknefoz.

Rule 9: To form a noun from a verb, add the suffix lek to the stem of the verb.

    Example: If longker is to write, then a writer is a longlek.

Rule 10: To form an adjective from a noun, substitute the suffix le for the suffix lek.

    Example: If pellek is beauty, then a beautiful male eagle is a pelle verlek and a beautiful female eagle is a pellenef verleknef. (Note the feminine suffix nef.)

Rule 11: To form an adverb from an adjective, add the suffix ki to the masculine form of the adjective. (Note that adverbs do not change their form to agree in gender or number with the word they modify.)

    Example: If pelle is beautiful, then beautifully is pelleki.

Rule 12: To form the possessive of a noun or pronoun, add the suffix ae to the noun or pronoun after any plural or feminine suffixes.

    Example: If a boglek is a dog, then a dog's collar is a boglekae collar.
                   If he is yev, then his book is yevae book.
                   If she is yevnef, then her book is yevnefae book.

Rule 13: To make a word negative, add the prefix fer to the correct affirmative form.

    Example: If an active male eagle is a sojle verlek, an inactive male eagle is a fersojle verlek.
                   If the dog barks is boglek nalem, then the dog does not bark is the boglek fernalem.

GLOSSARY OF GRAMMATICAL TERMS

This glossary will be available to you during the actual test, but it is recommended that you study the glossary before taking the test. The glossary contains basic grammatical concepts that apply to English, Spanish, and the Artificial Language. The glossary contains fairly extensive and comprehensive explanations of each grammatical concept. **The explanations in the actual test are not comprehensive. Consequently, it is particularly important that you study these explanations very carefully.**

Article: An article is a word that precedes a noun and determines whether it is a definite or indefinite noun; for instance the book, an object.

Adjective: An adjective is a word used to modify a noun or pronoun (for example, intelligent women). Generally, an adjective serves to answer questions such as: which, what kind of, how many. For example, (1) "This book" would be the adjectival answer to the question "which book?" (2) "a beautiful book" would be the adjectival answer to the question "what kind of book?" and (3) "several days" would be the adjectival answer to the question "how many days?"

In English, adjectives have only one form, regardless of the type of noun they modify. More specifically, whether a noun is feminine or masculine, singular or plural, the adjective used to modify it remains the same; for example, the adjective strong is exactly the same when it refers to one man, one woman, many women, or many men. By contrast, in both Spanish and the Artificial Language, the ending of the adjective is different if the adjective is modifying a singular masculine noun, a singular feminine noun, a plural feminine noun, or a plural masculine noun.

Adverb: An adverb is a word used to modify a verb. For example, the sentence "It was produced" could be modified to express where it was produced by saying "It was produced locally."

Generally, an adverb is used to answer the questions where (as in the example above), when (as for example, "he comes frequently"), how (as for example, "she thinks logically"). Adverbs sometimes are used to modify an adjective or another adverb. For example, in the sentence "She has a really beautiful mind," the adverb really modifies the adjective beautiful. In the sentence "She thinks very logically," the adverb very modifies the adverb logically. In the Artificial Language the only adverbs used are those which modify verbs. In the Spanish language, as well as in the English language, adverbs are used to modify verbs, adjectives, and other adverbs.

Gender: As a grammatical concept, gender refers to the classification of words according to whether they are masculine, feminine, or neuter.

As stated above, Spanish takes masculine or feminine endings for nouns, adjectives, and articles. The neuter form is used sometimes to express abstraction in a more emphatic manner. The neuter form is NOT used in the Artificial Language. Consequently, it is very important for you to remember that in the Artificial Language all nouns, adjectives, and articles take either a masculine or a feminine ending according to whether the sentence refers to a male or female.

Also, all nouns and adjectives in the Artificial Language were conceived (for the sake of simplicity) to be masculine. Thus, unless the feminine gender is specified in the sentence, the masculine gender is used always.

Infinitive: An infinitive is the general, abstract form of a verb; for example, to look, to think, to remember, to walk. Once the action expressed by a verb is attached to a specific subject (a person, animal, or thing), then we say the verb is "conjugated," or linked to that subject; for example, "he/she thinks," "the dog runs," "the table broke."

In contrast to the way that an infinitive in English is preceded by the word "to" (as in "to think"), in the Artificial Language (and in Spanish), infinitives are defined by their suffix. In the version of the Artificial Language used here, this ending (or suffix) is ker (in the actual test, the ending will be different).

Noun: A noun is a word which names a person, place, thing, or abstraction; for example, Lindsay, Chicago, tree, wisdom. A noun can refer to an individual (as in Lindsay, an individual person, or Chicago, an individual place) or to a set (as in "all stones," "all trees," "all cities").

Prefix: A prefix always occurs at the beginning of a word. It can be a single letter or a sequence of letters; for example, amoral, illegal, dysfunctional.

A prefix is the opposite of a suffix, which always occurs at the end of a word, but both serve to change the basic word in some way. For example, polite is the basic word (in this case an adjective) to express the concept of behavior that conforms to accepted social norms, while adding the prefix im and creating the word impolite transforms the word polite into its contradictory concept. You should note that in the Artificial Language a prefix is used to create a negative concept (see Rule 13). Such a rule mimics both Spanish and English, in both of which negation is usually expressed by using a negative prefix.

Pronoun: A pronoun is a word used in place of a noun; for example, "she" instead of "Lindsay," "they" instead of "the guards," "it" instead of "the stone," "himself/herself" instead of "the judge."

In both English and Spanish there is a difference between a pronoun that stands for the subject of an action (as in "He threw the stone," meaning that Lindsay threw the stone), and a pronoun that stands for the object of an action (as in "The stone was thrown at him," meaning that the stone was thrown at Lindsay). By contrast, in the Artificial Language used in this manual there is no grammatical difference between he and him, both being yev. Remember, however, that in the Artificial Language pronouns take feminine endings when the subject or object of the action is feminine. Accordingly, in the version of the Artificial Language given in this manual, both she (subject) and her (object) would be yevnef (i.e., yev plus the feminine suffix nef).

Suffix: A suffix always occurs at the end of a word. It can be a single letter or a sequence of letters, for example, creamy, readable, nicely. Unlike prefixes, suffixes often change the "part of speech" (i.e., the type of word). For example, in the case of creamy, the suffix y changes the noun <u>cream</u> into the adjective <u>creamy</u>, and in the case of <u>nicely</u>, the suffix <u>ly</u> changes the adjective <u>nice</u> into the adverb <u>nicely</u>.

In addition, suffixes are used to conjugate verbs (for example, to change the present tense into the past tense: you walk, you walk<u>ed</u>) and to create the plural form of nouns (for example, boy, boy<u>s</u>). In Spanish, suffixes are used for the same purposes, but they are used for other purposes too, such as creating plural forms for adjectives and changing the gender of a word.

In the Artificial Language, suffixes are used (1) to change the part of speech (for example, Rule 11 uses a suffix to change an adjective into an adverb), (2) to conjugate verbs (for example, Rules 6 and 7 use suffixes to express the present and past tenses), and (3) to create the plural form of nouns, pronouns, adjectives, and articles (Rule 2). In addition, the Artificial Language mimics Spanish in using a suffix to express gender.

You should study all the rules on suffixes in the Artificial Language, and you should practice using these rules, but you should NOT memorize them because (1) you will have them available to you at all times during the actual test, and (2) in the actual test, some of the suffixes and prefixes are different from the ones used in this practice test.

Verb: A verb is used to express either an action or a state of being. For example, "He <u>prepared</u> dinner" expresses the action of making all preparations for dinner, while "He <u>is</u> a citizen" expresses the state or condition of being a citizen.

A condition or "state of being" can be permanent or transitory. For example, "The agent's horse <u>is a bay mare</u>" expresses a permanent condition for the horse (being a bay mare), while "George <u>is at lunch</u>" expresses a transitory condition for George (being at lunch). The Spanish language, unlike English, has two different verbs to express permanent and transitory conditions, although the Artificial Language is akin to English rather than to Spanish in its use of a single verb to express any state of being.

When a verb is linked to a subject (i.e., "conjugated") it changes from the abstract infinitive form to a specific form such as a present tense or a past tense. The Artificial Language primarily uses only two tenses: the simple past tense and the simple present tense in the indicative mood (see Rules 6 and 7). (Verbs in the indicative mood express a <u>real</u> action or condition, whereas verbs in the subjunctive mood express <u>hypothetical</u> actions or conditions. The subjunctive mood does not exist in the Artificial Language, but it is very important in Spanish.)

You may find that the past participle is used in the test (see Rule 8). In that case, the present perfect tense (they <u>have crossed</u>) and the past perfect tense (they <u>had crossed</u>) will be used in the Artificial Language.

Be sure to apply the rules as directed in the test material. If no rule governing the past participle is listed in the actual test material, then the past participle is treated as a simple past tense.

PRACTICE TEST

<u>Directions for questions 1 through 20</u>

For each sentence, decide which words have been translated correctly. Use scratch paper to list each <u>numbered</u> word that is correctly translated into the Artificial Language. When you have finished listing the words that are correctly translated in sentences 1 through 20, select your answer according to the following instructions:

Mark:
   A) if <u>only</u> the word numbered 1 is correctly translated
   B) if <u>only</u> the word numbered 2 is correctly translated
   C) if <u>only</u> the word numbered 3 is correctly translated
   D) if <u>two</u> or <u>more</u> of the numbered words are correctly translated
   E) if <u>none</u> of the numbered words is correctly translated

Be sure to list only the <u>numbered</u> words which are <u>correctly</u> translated.

Study the sample question before going on to the test questions.

<u>Sample Sentence</u>	<u>Sample Translation</u>
He identifies the driver.	<u>Volle</u> <u>kalenim</u> wir <u>arlek</u>.
	1 2 3

The word numbered 1, <u>volle</u>, is incorrect since the translation of <u>volle</u> is <u>this</u>. The word <u>yev</u> should have been used.

The word numbered 2, <u>kalenim</u>, is also incorrect because the singular form <u>kalenem</u> should have been used.

The word numbered 3 is correct and should be written on your note paper. <u>Arlek</u> has been correctly formed from the infinitive <u>arker</u> (to drive) by applying Rules 9 and 4. Since the word numbered 3 has been identified as the only word translated correctly, the answer to the sample question is <u>C</u>.

Now go on with questions 1 through 20 and answer them in the manner indicated. <u>Be sure to record your answers on the separate answer sheet</u>.

<u>Sentence</u>	<u>Translation</u>
1. She is an alien.	<u>Yev</u> <u>synem</u> bexnef <u>huslek</u>.
	1 2 3
2. The guard is a friend.	<u>Wir</u> <u>bonlek</u> synem bex <u>kometlek</u>.
	1 2 3
3. The woman drove the jeep.	Wirnef <u>kapleknef</u> <u>arzotem</u> wir <u>daqlek</u>.
	1 2 3

	Sentence	Translation

4. That government is legal.

Velle <u>almanlek</u> <u>synzotim</u> <u>colleki</u>.
       1   2   3

5. The men and the women escaped.

Wiroz <u>kaplek</u> loa wirnefoz <u>kapleknef</u> <u>pirker</u>.
      1   2   3

6. The alien's friend injured him.

Wir <u>huslekae</u> kometlek <u>liazotim</u> <u>yevae</u>.
    1   2   3

7. This boy is from that country.

<u>Volle</u> ekaplek synem <u>mor</u> <u>volle</u> failek.
  1   2   3

8. Those were difficult inspections.

<u>Velle</u> synzotim <u>glasle</u> <u>zelkeroz</u>.
  1   2   3

9. Spies are disloyal.

<u>Tatleknef</u> <u>synzotem</u> <u>inlefer</u>.
    1   2   3

10. She was a skillful inspector.

Yevnef synzotem <u>bex</u> <u>janlenef</u> <u>zelnef</u>.
                1   2   3

11. Those aliens are not enemies of the government.

<u>Velle</u> huslekoz <u>synimfer</u> <u>avelekoz</u> quea wir almanlek.
  1   2   3

12. Guards have to identify illegal workers.

<u>Bonlekoz</u> tulim kalenker <u>fercolle</u> <u>friglekoz</u>.
   1   2   3

13. A friendly alien guarded the boys.

Bex <u>kometleki</u> huslek <u>bonzotem</u> wiroz <u>ekaplekoz</u>.
     1   2   3

14. She is a loyal and skillful guard.

<u>Yevnef</u> synem bexnef <u>inle</u> loa <u>janle</u> bonleknef.
  1   2   3

15. These women work illegally.

<u>Volleoz</u> kapleknefoz <u>frigim</u> <u>fercollekinef</u>.
  1   2   3

16. The illegal papers were identified.

Wiroz <u>fercolle</u> <u>trenedlekoz</u> <u>synim</u> kalentooz.
      1   2   3

17. Those women are not aliens from that country.

Vellenefoz kapleknefoz <u>fersynem</u> <u>huslekoz</u> mor velle <u>failek</u>.
                  1   2   3

18. Spies are disloyal enemies of their countries.

<u>Tatlekoz</u> synim <u>ferinle</u> avelekoz quea <u>yevae</u> failekoz.
   1   2   3

19. The illegal aliens were not injured.

Wiroz <u>fercolle</u> huslekoz <u>synimfer</u> <u>liatooz</u>.
      1   2   3

20. The river borders the country, and to cross the river is not legal.

Wir browlek regem wir failek, loa <u>chonker</u> wir browlek
                                          1

<u>synem</u> <u>fercolle</u>.
  2   3

Directions for questions 21 through 30

For each question in this group, select the one of the five suggested choices that correctly translates the underlined word or group of words into the Artificial Language.

Sample question: There is the boy.

A) bex kaplek   B) wir kaplek   C) wir ekaplek   D) velle ekaplek   E) bex ekaplek

Response Option C is the correct translation of the underlined words, the boy. Now read the following paragraph and choose the correct translation for the words or groups of words that are underlined.

Paragraph

The men and women who patrol and guard the border have a complex and difficult job. They have to deal with
              21   22
both friendly and unfriendly aliens, as well as with well-trained and skillful spies, who are often dangerous.
                             23   24
They have to inspect and identify complex governmental papers that are written in various foreign languages,
            25   26
and they have to make difficult decisions, frequently alone and away from their stations. This country's
                                                                               27   28
borders are skillfully guarded and kept secure by these loyal women and these loyal men.
                             29   30

21. A) kaplekoz loa kaplekferoz
     B) kaplekoz loa kapleknefoz
     C) kaplekae loa kapleknefae
     D) kaplekae loa kaplekferae
     E) kaplekoz bex kaplekferoz

22. A) bonimoz wir reglek
     B) bonimoz wir reglekoz
     C) bonem wir reglek
     D) bonker wir reglek
     E) bonim wir reglek

23. A) ferkometlekkioz huslekoz
     B) ferkometlekki huslekki
     C) ferkometleoz huslekoz
     D) ferkometlekoz huslekoz
     E) ferkometlekkioz huslekkioz

24. A) janle tatlekoz
     B) janle tatlek
     C) janleoz tatlekoz
     D) janleoz tatkeroz
     E) janle tatkeroz

25. A) yevoz tulim zelkerim
     B) yevoz tulem zelker
     C) yevoz tulzotim zelker
     D) yevoz tulzotim zelkerim
     E) yevoz tulim zelker

26. A) almanleoz trenedlekoz
     B) almanlek trenedlek
     C) almanlek trenedlekoz
     D) almanlekoz trenedlekoz
     E) almanle trenedlekoz

27. A) lexkeroz
     B) lexlekae
     C) lexkerae
     D) lexlekoz
     E) lexleoz

28. A) volle failekae
     B) volleae failekae
     C) volle failek
     D) volleae failek
     E) volle faileae

29. A) janlekioz bonzotim
     B) janleki bontooz
     C) janleki bonto
     D) janlekioz bonzotem
     E) janleki bonlekki

30. A) volleoz inlenef kapleknefoz
     B) vollenefoz inlenefoz kapleknefoz
     C) volleoz inle kapleknefoz
     D) vollenefoz inlenef kapleknefoz
     E) vollenefoz inle kapleknefoz

Directions for questions 31 through 42

For this group of questions, select the one response option that is the correct translation of the English word or words in parentheses. You should translate the entire sentence in order to determine what form should be used.

Sample question: (The man) synem bex avelek.

A) Bex kaplek   B) Bex ekaplek   C) Loa kaplek   D) Wir kaplek   E) Wirlek kaplek

Since <u>Wir kaplek</u> is the only one of these expressions that means <u>the man</u>, D is the correct answer to the sample question. Now answer questions 31 through 44.

31. Velleoz (boys escaped).
   A) ekaplekoz pirzotim
   B) ekaplekoz pirkerim
   C) ekaplekim pirzotim
   D) ekaplekim pirkerim
   E) ekaplekae pirzotim

32. Wirnefoz kapleknefoz (drove skillfully).
   A) arzotnefim janlekinef
   B) arzotnefim janlekinefoz
   C) arzotim janlekinef
   D) arzotim janleki
   E) arzotim janlekinefoz

33. Yevoz liazotim (her friend).
   A) yevnefae kometlek
   B) yevnef kometlek
   C) yevae kometlek
   D) yevnefae kometleknef
   E) yevnef kometleknef

34. (She was) mor velle failek.
   A) Yevnef synzotim
   B) Yevnef synzotem
   C) Yevnef synzotnefim
   D) Yevnef synzotnefem
   E) Yevnef synim

35. Wiroz (women's papers) synim colleoz.
   A) kapleknefae trenedlekoz
   B) kapleknefozae trenedlekoz
   C) kapleknefae trenedlekae
   D) kapleknefozae trenedlekozae
   E) kapleknefozae trenedleknefoz

36. Yevnef (has to cross) velle browlek.
   A) tulnefem chonkernef
   B) tulemnef chonkernef
   C) tulem chonkerem
   D) tulkerem chonker
   E) tulem chonker

37. Yevoz (work illegally).
   A) frigem fercolleki
   B) frigim colleki
   C) frigim fercolleki
   D) frigim fercolleim
   E) frigem fercolleem

38. Wirnefoz ferinlenefoz kapleknefoz (had spied).
   A) tulker tatker
   B) tulim tatkernefoz
   C) tulem tattonefoz
   D) tulzotim tatto
   E) tulzotem tatker

39. (That government's spies) synzotim avelekoz.
   A) Velle almanlekae tatlekoz
   B) Velle almanlekoz tatlekoz
   C) Volle almanlekae tatlekoz
   D) Volle almanlekozae tatlekoz
   E) Volle almanlekoz tatlekoz

40. Yevnef (is not an illegal) husleknef.
   A) fersynem bex fercolle
   B) fersynem bex fercollenef
   C) fersynem bexnef fercolle
   D) synem bex colle
   E) fersynem bexnef fercollenef

41. Yev chonzotem wir (guard's station illegally).
   A) bonlekem lexlek fercolleki
   B) bonlekae lexlek fercolleki
   C) bonlekem lexlekem fercolleki
   D) bonlek lexlek fercolleki
   E) bonlekae lexlekae fercollekiae

42. Wiroz (inspected) kaplekoz chonzotim wir reglek.
   A) zelzotim
   B) zelim
   C) zelto
   D) zelzotoz
   E) zeltooz

<u>Directions for questions 43 through 50</u>

For the last group of questions (43 through 50), select the one of the five suggested answers which is the correct form of the <u>underlined</u> expression as it is used in the sentence. At the end of the sentence you will find instructions in parentheses telling you which form to use. In some sentences you will be asked to supply the correct form of two or more expressions. In this case, the instructions for these expressions are presented consecutively in the parentheses and are separated by a dash (for example, "past tense—adverb"). Be sure to translate the entire sentence before selecting your answer.

<u>Sample question:</u>   Yev <u>bonker</u> wir browlek. (present tense)

   A) bonzotem   B) bonzotim   C) boneim   D) bonim   E) bonem

Choices A and B are incorrect because they are in the past tense. Choice C is misspelled. Choice D is in the present tense, but it too is incorrect because the subject of the sentence is singular and therefore takes a verb with a singular rather than a plural ending. E is the answer to the sample question. When you understand what you are to do, answer the rest of the questions in the test.

43. Wiroz huslekoz <u>tulker chonker</u> wir browlek. (present perfect plural verb)

    A) tulim chonim
    B) tultooz chontooz
    C) tulim chonto
    D) tulzotim chonzotim
    E) tulzotim chontooz

44. Yevnefoz fersynim <u>inle</u>. (negative plural feminine adjective)

    A) inlefer
    B) ferinlenefoz
    C) ferinlenef
    D) ferinleoz
    E) ferinlenoz

45. Yevnef <u>arker janle</u> mor wir lexlek. (past tense—adverb)

    A) arzotnef—janleki
    B) arzotem—janleki
    C) arzotem—janlenef
    D) arzotnef—janlenefki
    E) arzotem—janlenefki

46. <u>Volle</u> <u>kaplek</u> trenedlekoz synzotim mor yevnefae failek.
    (feminine plural adjective—feminine plural possessive noun)

    A) Vollenefoz—kapleknefozae
    B) Volleoznef—kapleknefozae
    C) Volleoz—kapleknefae
    D) Vollenefoz—kapleknefoz
    E) Vollenefoz—kapleknefaeoz

47. Wirnefoz kapleknefoz synzotim <u>zelker</u>, loa <u>yev</u> degzotim wir tatlek.
    (feminine plural noun—feminine plural pronoun)

    A) zellekoz—yevnefoz
    B) zelkeroz—yevnefoz
    C) zellekoz—yevoz
    D) zelkeroz—yevoz
    E) zelleknefoz—yevnefoz

48. Wirnef <u>avelek</u> synzotem <u>kalenker</u>.
    (feminine singular noun—past participle as predicate)

    A) aveleknef—kalentonef
    B) aveleknef—kalenzotem
    C) avelek—kalento
    D) aveleknef—kalenzotnef
    E) avelek—kalenker

49. Vellenefoz <u>colle</u> <u>huslek</u> <u>degker</u> liazotim wiroz ekaplekoz.
    (negative feminine plural adjective—possessive feminine plural noun—plural noun)

    A) fercollenef—huslekae—deglekoz
    B) fercolle—huslekae—deglekoz
    C) fercolle—husleknefae—deglekoz
    D) fercollenefoz—husleknefozae—deglekoz
    E) fercollenefoz—husleknefozae—degleknefoz

50. Wiroz <u>liaker</u> ekaplekoz synzotim <u>kometlek</u>.
    (plural past participle adjective—negative plural adjective)

    A) lialeoz— kometleoz
    B) liatooz—ferkometleoz
    C) liato—ferkometle
    D) liaim—ferkometleoz
    E) liatooz—kometleoz

RATIONALE FOR EACH RESPONSE CHOICE

A rationale, or justification, is provided below for each response choice in the practice test, including both correct and incorrect response choices. The purpose of these rationales is to help you to understand <u>why</u> each response choice is right or wrong, and, consequently, to help you to familiarize yourself more and more with the structures of the Artificial Language.

Question 1   Only the word numbered 2 is correct, so the answer is B.

The word numbered 1, <u>yev</u>, is incorrect because it means <u>he</u>, not <u>she</u>. Rule 1 states that to form the feminine singular of a pronoun, you have to add the suffix <u>nef</u> to the masculine singular form. Consequently, the correct pronoun for <u>she</u> is <u>yevnef</u>.

The word numbered 2, <u>synem</u>, is correct. According to Rules 4 and 6, to form the present tense of a verb, you should add the suffix <u>em</u> to the stem of the verb when the verb has a singular subject (as is the case here). Note also that according to Rule 4, the stem of a verb is obtained by omitting the suffix <u>ker</u> from the infinitive form of the verb. Note also that according to Rule 5, all subjects and their verbs must agree in number; thus, if the subject is singular, the verb must be in the singular form.

The word numbered 3, <u>huslek</u>, is incorrect. According to Rule 1, a feminine noun must take the ending <u>nef</u>. Accordingly, the word numbered 3 should have been <u>husleknef</u>.

Question 2   Since all three words are correct, the answer is D.

The word numbered 1, <u>wir</u>, is correct. The vocabulary lists state that <u>wir</u> is the translation for <u>the</u>. Since the feminine gender is not specified, <u>wir</u> does not take a feminine ending.

The word numbered 2, <u>bonlek</u>, is correct. According to Rule 9, in order to form a noun from a verb, the suffix <u>lek</u> should be added to the stem of the infinitive. The infinitive (as it appears in the vocabulary list) is <u>bonker</u>, and its stem is <u>bon</u> (note that <u>all</u> infinitives in the vocabulary list have the suffix <u>ker</u> and are distinguished only by their respective stems).

The word numbered 3, <u>kometlek</u>, is correct. This is the word for <u>friend</u> as it appears in the vocabulary lists. Since the feminine gender is not specified in the sentence, <u>kometlek</u> does not take a feminine ending.

Question 3   Since all three words are correct, the answer is D.

The word numbered 1, <u>kapleknef</u>, is correct. According to Rule 1, the feminine singular of a noun is formed by adding the suffix <u>nef</u> to the masculine singular. Accordingly, to form the word <u>woman</u>, the suffix <u>nef</u> should be added to the word <u>kaplek</u> (man).

The word numbered 2, <u>arzotem</u>, is correct. According to Rule 4, the stem of the infinitive <u>to drive</u> is <u>ar</u> (since the infinitive form is <u>arker</u> in the vocabulary list). Since, according to Rule 7, the past tense is formed by adding the suffix zot to the stem of the verb and then adding the suffix em when the verb is singular, the correct translation of drove is arzotem.

The word numbered 3, daqlek, is the correct translation for jeep in the vocabulary lists.

Question 4   Since only the word numbered 1 is correct, the answer is A.

The word numbered 1, almanlek, is the correct translation for the word government in the vocabulary list.

The word numbered 2, synzotim, is incorrect. The correct way to form the present tense singular according to Rule 6 is to add the suffix em to the stem of the verb. Accordingly, the correct translation for is would be synem. The erroneous word synzotim is actually the past tense in the plural form were (see Rule 7).

The word numbered 3, colleki, is incorrect. The correct translation for the word legal, which is an adjective, is colle (see vocabulary lists). The erroneous word colleki is actually the adverb legally, which is formed by adding the suffix ki to the adjectival form (see Rule 11).

Question 5   Since none of the numbered words is correct, the answer is E.

The word numbered 1, kaplek is incorrect. Kaplek is the word for the singular noun man. Since the word men is a plural noun, the correct translation according to Rule 2 would have been kaplekoz. As Rule 2 states, in the Artificial Language the plural of nouns is formed by adding the suffix oz to the correct singular form.

The word numbered 2, kapleknef, is incorrect. Kapleknef is the word for the singular noun woman. Consequently, the word kapleknef correctly includes the suffix nef for the feminine form (Rule 1), but incorrectly neglects the suffix oz for the plural form (Rule 2). The correct translation of women is kapleknefoz.

The word numbered 3, pirker, is incorrect. Pirker (to escape) is the infinitive form of the verb, whereas the sentence calls for the past tense escaped. To form the past tense (Rule 7) the suffix zot should be added to the stem of the verb, and then the suffix im should be added when the verb refers to a plural subject (men and women). Accordingly, the correct translation is pirzotim.

Question 6   Since only the word numbered 1 is correct, the answer is A.

The word numbered 1, huslekae, is correct. Since alien's is a possessive form, the word huslek (alien) must take the possessive suffix ae (Rule 12).

The word numbered 2, liazotim, is incorrect. Liazotim correctly applies Rule 4 to form the stem of the verb and correctly applies the suffix for the past tense, zot, but it incorrectly applies the plural suffix im. The correct translation for injured in this sentence would be liazotem since the verb refers to a singular subject and therefore takes the suffix em (see Rule 7).

The word numbered 3, yevae, is incorrect. The possessive ending yevae would apply to the possessive pronoun his, whereas the pronoun used in the sentence is him. According to the vocabulary list, the translation for him is yev. Accordingly, yev should have been used in the sentence.

Question 7   Since two of the numbered words are correct, the answer is D.

The word numbered 1, volle, is correct. According to the vocabulary lists, the correct translation for this is volle.

The word numbered 2, mor, is correct. According to the vocabulary lists, the correct translation for from is mor.

You should note that it is not always necessary to apply the grammatical rules, as is the case with the two words above. In the case of these words, it is sufficient to consult the vocabulary lists. It is necessary to apply the grammatical rules only when the word in question cannot be used exactly as it appears in the vocabulary lists.

The word numbered 3, volle, is incorrect. According to the vocabulary lists, the correct translation for that is velle (volle means this, as seen in the case of the word numbered 1, above).

Question 8   Since none of the numbered words is correct, the answer is E.

The word numbered 1, velle, is incorrect. The correct translation of those would be velleoz, since those is the plural of that and, according to Rule 2, the plural form for pronouns must take the suffix oz.

The word numbered 2, glasle, is incorrect. Glasle means difficult (as can be seen in the vocabulary lists), but according to Rule 2 adjectives take the ending oz when they are modifying a plural noun. Since the adjective difficult in the sentence is modifying the plural noun inspections, it must take the suffix oz. Accordingly, the correct form to use is glasleoz. (It is very important for you to bear in mind at all times that in the Artificial Language, as discussed in the section on grammatical rules, and as specifically dictated by Rules 1 and 3, nouns, pronouns, adjectives, and articles take plural and feminine suffixes in plural and feminine contexts. These transformations are akin to those of neo-Latin languages, including Spanish.)

The word numbered 3, zelkeroz, is incorrect. According to Rule 9, in order to form a noun from a verb, the suffix lek should be added to the stem of the verb (in this case zel, which according to Rule 4 is the stem of the infinitive zelker, to inspect). Thus, the noun inspection (singular) is zellek; but in the sentence this noun appears in the plural (inspections). Consequently, according to Rule 2, zellek must take the ending oz, thus making it the plural zellekoz.

Question 9   Since none of the numbered words is correct, the answer is E.

The word numbered 1, tatleknef, is incorrect. Tatleknef is the correct word for a female spy (Rules 4, 9, and 1) whereas the word numbered 1 in the sentence refers to spies, in the plural and with no specification as to gender. Therefore, the correct translation would be <u>tatlekoz</u>, which first forms a noun (tatlek) from the infinitive verb (<u>tatker</u>) according to Rules 4 and 9, and then forms the plural <u>tatlekoz</u> according to Rule 2.

The word numbered 2, <u>synzotem</u>, is incorrect. The verb in the English sentence is a present tense in the plural form (<u>are</u>). The correct translation in this case must be <u>synim</u>, according to Rule 6, which states that, in order to form the present tense in the plural form, you should add the suffix <u>im</u> to the stem of the infinitive (which is itself formed by applying Rule 4).

The word numbered 3, <u>inlefer</u>, is incorrect. According to Rule 13, the adjective <u>disloyal</u> must be formed by adding the negative prefix <u>fer</u> to the adjective <u>inle</u> (<u>loyal</u>). The word numbered 3, <u>inlefer</u>, erroneously uses <u>fer</u> as a negative suffix rather than as a negative prefix. In addition, the adjective must have a plural ending according to Rule 2, since it refers to the plural noun <u>spies</u>. Consequently, the correct translation must be <u>ferinleoz</u>.

Question 10   Since only the word numbered 2 is correct, the answer is B.

The word numbered 1, <u>bex</u>, is incorrect. In the Artificial Language the article <u>bex</u> (in English <u>a/an</u>) takes a feminine ending (see Rules 1 and 3). The correct word is <u>bexnef</u>.

The word numbered 2, <u>janlenef</u>, is correct. <u>Janle</u> (<u>skillful</u>) is an adjective, and as such must take a feminine ending when referring to a feminine subject (see Rules 1 and 3).

The word numbered 3, <u>zelnef</u>, is incorrect. Since it is a noun (<u>inspector</u> in English), it must first take the ending <u>lek</u>—this is required by Rules 4 and 9, which state that to form a noun from a verb the suffix <u>lek</u> should replace the infinitive suffix <u>ker</u> (note that the infinitive form appears in the vocabulary lists: <u>zelker</u>). Once the noun (<u>zellek</u>) has been formed, then the feminine suffix <u>nef</u> must be added because the sentence has a feminine subject. Accordingly, the correct word would be <u>zelleknef</u>.

Question 11   Since only the word numbered 3 is correct, the answer is C.

The word numbered 1, <u>velle</u>, is incorrect. <u>Velle</u> means <u>that</u>, whereas the word in the sentence is the plural <u>those</u>. Accordingly, <u>velle</u> must appear in the plural, which would be <u>velleoz</u> (see Rule 2, which states that the plural of adjectives must be formed by adding the suffix <u>oz</u> to the singular form).

The word numbered 2, <u>synimfer</u>, is incorrect. The first portion of the word <u>synim</u> is the correct form for <u>are</u> in the plural (see Rules 4 and 6), but the negative form <u>fer</u> must be used as a prefix rather than as a suffix (see Rule 13). Accordingly, the correct form for <u>are not</u> in the plural must be <u>fersynim</u>.

The word numbered 3, <u>avelekoz</u>, is correct. According to the vocabulary lists, the correct translation of the noun <u>enemy</u> is <u>avelek</u>, and according to Rule 2, the plural of nouns is formed by adding the suffix <u>oz</u> to the singular.

Question 12   Since two of the numbered words are correct, the answer is D.

The word numbered 1, <u>bonlekoz</u>, is correct. <u>Bonlekoz</u> (which means <u>guards</u>) is formed by first changing the infinitive verb <u>to guard</u> (<u>bonker</u>) into the singular noun <u>bonlek</u> (see Rules 4 and 9, which state that to form a noun from a verb you should add the suffix <u>lek</u> to the stem of the verb). Next, in order to make the noun plural (<u>guards</u>), the suffix <u>oz</u> should be added to the singular form.

The word numbered 2, <u>fercolle</u>, is incorrect. According to Rule 13, the adjective <u>illegal</u> must be formed by adding the prefix <u>fer</u> to the adjective <u>colle</u> (legal). According to Rules 3 and 2, the ending <u>oz</u> must be added to make the adjective plural because it is modifying a plural noun (<u>workers</u>). Accordingly, the correct word would be <u>fercolleoz</u>.

The word numbered 3, <u>friglekoz</u>, is correct. The first portion of the noun, <u>friglek</u>, means <u>worker</u>; you form this noun (according to Rules 4 and 9) by adding the suffix <u>lek</u> to the stem of the infinitive <u>frigker</u> (<u>to work</u>). Next, according to Rule 2, in order to make the noun plural, you add the suffix <u>oz</u> to the singular.

Question 13   Since two of the numbered words are correct, the answer is D.

The word numbered 1, <u>kometleki</u>, is incorrect. <u>Kometleki</u> uses the adverbial ending <u>ki</u>, whereas "friendly" is modifying the noun "alien" and is therefore, by definition, an adjective. The adjective is formed from the noun <u>kometlek</u> (found in the vocabulary lists) by changing the suffix <u>lek</u> to the suffix <u>le</u> (see Rule 10). Accordingly, the correct word would be <u>kometle</u>.

The word numbered 2, <u>bonzotem</u>, is correct. <u>Bonzotem</u> (<u>guarded</u>) is the past tense of the verb <u>to guard</u> (<u>bonker</u>). According to Rules 4 and 7, <u>bonzotem</u> is formed by adding the suffix <u>zot</u> to the stem of the infinitive (<u>bon</u>). Next, according to Rule 7, since the sentence is about a singular subject ("a friendly alien"), the suffix <u>em</u> is added to the past tense, thus forming <u>bonzotem</u>.

The word numbered 3, <u>ekaplekoz</u>, is correct. The noun <u>ekaplek</u> means <u>boy</u>, but since the sentence refers to <u>boys</u> in the plural, the correct noun in the Artificial Language is <u>ekaplekoz</u> (according to Rule 2, the plural of nouns is formed by adding the suffix <u>oz</u> to the singular form).

Question 14   Since only the word numbered 1 is correct, the answer is A.

The word numbered 1, <u>yevnef</u>, is correct. According to Rule 1, the pronoun <u>she</u> is formed by adding the suffix <u>nef</u> to the masculine pronoun <u>yev</u> (<u>he</u>).

The word numbered 2, <u>inle</u>, is incorrect. Since the subject of the sentence (<u>she</u>) is feminine, the adjective <u>inle</u> (<u>loyal</u>) must take the feminine ending <u>nef</u> (see Rules 1 and 3), thus making it <u>inlenef</u>.

Similarly, the word numbered 3, <u>janle</u>, is incorrect because the adjective <u>janle</u> (<u>skillful</u>) must take the feminine ending <u>nef</u>, thus making it <u>janlenef</u>.

Question 15   Since only the word numbered 2 is correct, the answer is B.

The word numbered 1, <u>volleoz</u>, is incorrect. <u>Volleoz</u> (these) is in the masculine form. Since the sentence is about a feminine subject (<u>women</u>), you must apply Rules 1 and 3, according to which adjectives (such as <u>these</u>) modifying a feminine noun (such as <u>women</u>) must take the ending <u>nef</u> before taking the plural ending <u>oz</u> (see Rule 2). Accordingly, the correct form for <u>these</u> in this sentence would be <u>vollenefoz</u>.

The word numbered 2, <u>frigim</u>, is correct. According to Rules 4 and 6, the present tense of a verb is formed by adding the suffix <u>im</u> to the stem of the infinitive when the verb has a plural subject (as is the case in this sentence: <u>women work</u>).

The word numbered 3, <u>fercollekinef</u>, is incorrect. According to Rule 11, in order to form an adverb from an adjective, you should add the suffix <u>ki</u> to the adjectival form. Thus, the adverb <u>colleki</u> (<u>legally</u>) is formed by adding the suffix <u>ki</u> to the adjective <u>colle</u> (<u>legal</u>). Next, when the word is negative, it takes the prefix <u>fer</u> (see Rule 13); accordingly, the adverb <u>colleki</u> must take the prefix <u>fer</u>, thus becoming the negative adverb <u>fercolleki</u> (<u>illegally</u>). Finally, the word <u>fercolleki</u>, being an adverb, must never take the feminine ending <u>nef</u>. As stated in Rule 11, adverbs do not change their form according to gender. The reason is that adverbs, by definition, modify verbs, which are, also by definition, genderless (see the discussion on verbs and adverbs in the glossary).

Question 16   Since only the word numbered 2 is correct, the answer is B.

The word numbered 1, <u>fercolle</u>, is incorrect. The negative form for the term <u>illegal</u> is correctly formed according to Rule 13 by adding the prefix <u>fer</u> to the adjective <u>colle</u> (<u>legal</u>), but in this sentence the adjective <u>illegal</u> is modifying the plural noun <u>papers</u> (<u>trenedlekoz</u>) and must consequently take the plural ending <u>oz</u>, thus forming the plural adjective <u>fercolleoz</u> (Rules 2 and 3).

The word numbered 2, <u>trenedlekoz</u>, is correct. The singular noun <u>paper</u> (<u>trenedlek</u>) can be found in the vocabulary lists. Its plural is formed, according to Rule 2, by adding the suffix <u>oz</u> to the singular form, thus forming <u>trenedlekoz</u>.

The word numbered 3, <u>synim</u>, is incorrect. The plural form of the past tense (<u>were</u>) is formed according to Rules 4 and 7 by adding the suffix <u>zot</u> to the stem of the verb (<u>syn</u>) and then adding the suffix <u>im</u> for the plural. Accordingly, the correct translation for <u>were</u> would be <u>synzotim</u>.

Question 17   Since only the word numbered 3 is correct, the answer is C.

The word numbered 1, <u>fersynem</u>, is incorrect. The verb (<u>are</u>) is a plural verb and, consequently, according to Rule 6, it must take the suffix <u>im</u>, rather than the suffix <u>em</u>. On the other hand, the use of the negative prefix (<u>fer</u>) is correct, since according to Rule 13 the prefix <u>fer</u> should be added to the affirmative form in order to make a word negative. Accordingly, the correct word for <u>are not</u> is <u>fersynim</u>.

The word numbered 2, huslekoz, is incorrect. According to the vocabulary lists, huslek means alien, and, according to Rule 2, the plural of a noun is formed by adding the suffix oz, but since the subject of the sentence is feminine (women), the suffix nef must be added to the noun before making it plural (see Rules 1 and 2). Accordingly, the correct word is husleknefoz.

The word numbered 3, failek, is correct. Failek is the word that appears in the vocabulary lists for country.

Question 18   Since only the word numbered 1 is correct, the answer is A.

The word numbered 1, tatlekoz, is correct. According to Rules 4 and 9, in order to form a noun from a verb, the suffix lek should be added to the stem of the infinitive. Accordingly, in order to form the singular noun spy, the suffix lek should be added to the stem tat of the infinitive tatker (to spy). Next, since the sentence contains the noun in the plural form, spies, tatlek must be transformed into its plural form. According to Rule 2, in order to form the plural of a noun, the suffix oz must be added to the singular. Consequently, the correct translation for spies is tatlekoz.

The word numbered 2, ferinle, is incorrect. According to the vocabulary lists, the correct translation for the adjective loyal is inle, and according to Rule 13, the negative form, disloyal, is formed by adding the prefix fer to the affirmative form (thus forming the word ferinle). However, in the context of the sentence, ferinle is incorrect because it is a singular form, whereas the adjective in the sentence is modifying the plural noun avelekoz (enemies), thus necessitating the plural ending oz (see Rules 2 and 3). The correct word, therefore, would be ferinleoz.

The word numbered 3, yevae, is incorrect. According to the vocabulary lists, the pronoun yev means he or him; and the ending ae, according to Rule 12, is used to form the possessive form of a pronoun. Accordingly, yevae would be the possessive pronoun his, rather than the plural their that appears in the sentence. Their is formed by first adding the suffix oz to the singular, thus forming the pronoun they (yevoz), and then adding the possessive ae, thus forming the possessive pronoun their (yevozae).

Question 19   Since only the word numbered 3 is correct, the answer is C.

The word numbered 1, fercolle, is incorrect. According to the vocabulary lists, colle means legal. According to Rule 13, the negative form fercolle (illegal) is formed by adding the negative prefix fer to the affirmative. However, the adjective illegal is modifying a plural noun (aliens) in the sentence. Consequently, the adjective fercolle must take the plural ending oz, thus forming the word fercolleoz (Rules 2 and 3).

The word numbered 2, synimfer, is incorrect. Synim is the present tense plural are, whereas the sentence has the verb in the past tense, were. According to Rules 4 and 7 the past tense is formed by adding the suffix zot to the stem of the infinitive and then adding the suffix im when the verb is in the plural form. Accordingly, the correct translation of were would be synzotim. Lastly, since the sentence has this verb in the negative form, were not, the prefix fer must be added to the verb (Rule 13), thus forming <u>fersynzotim</u>. (Note that the sentence in question 19 incorrectly uses <u>fer</u> as a suffix, rather than as a prefix.)

The word numbered 3, <u>liatooz</u>, is correct. In this sentence, <u>liatooz</u> is a past participle, which is formed according to Rule 8. First, the suffix <u>to</u> should be added to the stem of the infinitive to make the verb a past participle. Next, the suffiz <u>oz</u> should be added to the past participle because the participle is used as a predicate to modify the masculine plural noun <u>aliens</u>.

Question 20   Since only the word numbered 1 is correct, the answer is A.

The word numbered 1, <u>chonker</u>, is correct. According to the vocabulary lists, <u>chonker</u> is the infinitive form of the verb <u>to cross</u>.

The word numbered 2, <u>synem</u>, is incorrect. The verb <u>synem</u> means <u>is</u> (it is formed by adding the suffix <u>em</u> to the stem <u>syn</u>, as indicated in Rules 4 and 6). In the sentence, however, the verb is negated (<u>is not</u>). According to Rule 13, a word is negated by adding the prefix <u>fer</u> to the word. Consequently, the correct translation for <u>is not</u> is <u>fersynem</u>.

The word numbered 3, <u>fercolle</u>, is incorrect. According to the vocabulary lists, <u>colle</u> means <u>legal</u>. By applying Rule 13, we can make the word negative if we add the prefix <u>fer</u>, thus forming <u>fercolle</u>. However, this word means <u>illegal</u>, whereas in the sentence the adjective <u>legal</u> is not negated. What is negated is the verb <u>is</u>. Consequently, the correct translation of <u>is not legal</u> is <u>fersynem colle</u>, rather than <u>synem fercolle</u> (which would be literally <u>is illegal</u>). Whereas logically the two phrases have the same meaning, structurally (grammatically) they are not the same.

Question 21   The answer is B: <u>kaplekoz loa kapleknefoz</u>

First, the plural noun <u>men</u> is formed, according to Rule 2, by adding the suffix <u>oz</u> to the singular form of the noun <u>kaplek</u>. Accordingly, the correct word is <u>kaplekoz</u>. *Second*, the word <u>and</u> (<u>loa</u>) is found in the vocabulary lists. *Third*, the plural noun <u>women</u> is formed, according to Rules 1 and 2, by first adding the feminine suffix <u>nef</u> to the singular masculine form of the noun (<u>kaplek</u>) and then adding the suffix <u>oz</u> for the plural. Accordingly, the correct word is <u>kapleknefoz</u>.

Among the incorrect choices, response A incorrectly uses the negative <u>fer</u> instead of the feminine <u>nef</u>; response C incorrectly uses the possessive form <u>ae</u> instead of the plural form <u>oz</u>; response D incorrectly uses both the negative <u>fer</u> and the possessive <u>ae</u>; and response E incorrectly uses the negative <u>fer</u> and the article <u>bex</u> (<u>a, an</u>).

Question 22   The answer is E: <u>bonim wir reglek</u>

First, you must form the present tense of the verb <u>to guard</u> (<u>bonker</u>). According to Rules 4 and 6, the present tense of a verb is formed by omitting the infinitive suffix <u>ker</u> and replacing it with the suffix <u>im</u> when the subject is plural. Since the subject of this sentence is plural (<u>men and women</u>, i.e., <u>they</u>), the verb should take the plural suffix. Accordingly, the correct form is bonim. **Second**, the article the is translated as wir, according to the vocabulary lists. **Third**, the noun border (reglek) is formed according to Rule 9 by adding the suffix lek to the stem of the verb.

Among the incorrect choices, response A incorrectly applies Rule 2 to the verb by adding the suffix oz to the plural verb bonim. Rule 2 is only used to form the plural of nouns, pronouns, adjectives, and articles, NOT verbs. Response B also incorrectly applies Rule 2 to the verb, and, in addition, applies Rule 2 to the noun reglek (border), thus incorrectly making it the plural reglekoz (borders). Response C incorrectly uses the singular form of the verb (bonem), and response D incorrectly uses the infinitive form of the verb (bonker).

Question 23   The answer is C: ferkometleoz huslekoz

First, the word ferkometleoz (unfriendly in the plural form) is formed by applying Rules 10, 13, 3, and 2. Rule 10 tells you that to form an adjective from a noun you should use the suffix le, instead of the suffix lek. Hence you change the noun kometlek (friend), which appears in the vocabulary lists, to the adjective kometle; but since the adjective is negative in the sentence, and since it is modifying the plural noun aliens, you must also apply Rule 13 (thus adding the negative prefix fer) and Rules 3 and 2, thus adding the plural suffix oz. **Second**, the word huslekoz (aliens) is formed by applying Rule 2, according to which you must add the suffix oz to form the plural of a noun.

Among the incorrect choices, responses A, B, and E erroneously apply the rule to form adverbs (Rule 11) to the noun kometlek. In addition, responses B and E make the same error with the noun huslek. Response D erroneously applies the plural oz to the noun form ferkometlek (non-friend), rather than to the correct adjectival form (ferkometle).

Question 24   The answer is C: janleoz tatlekoz

First, the word janleoz (skillful in the plural form) is formed by applying Rules 3 and 2, according to which the suffix oz must be added to the adjective janle (skillful) because it is modifying the plural noun spies. **Second**, the word tatlekoz (spies) is formed by applying Rules 4, 9, and 2, according to which in order to form a noun from a verb you should add the suffix lek to the stem of the infinitive and, next, you should add the suffix oz to make the noun plural.

Among the incorrect choices, responses A, B, and E incorrectly neglect Rules 3 and 2 by using the singular adjective janle. In addition, response B fails to use the correct plural for spies; and responses D and E neglect Rule 9 to form a noun and instead use the infinitive to spy (tatker) with the plural ending oz (which, according to Rule 2, is only for nouns, pronouns, adjectives, and articles).

Question 25   The answer is E: yevoz tulim zelker

First, the pronoun yevoz (they) is formed according to Rule 2 by adding the plural suffix to the singular pronoun yev (he). (Remember that all nouns and pronouns, unless referring to a specifically feminine subject, are assumed to be masculine.) **Second**, the verb tulim (have in the plural present tense) is formed according to Rules 4 and 6 by adding the plural suffix <u>im</u> to the stem of the infinitive. ***Third***, the infinitive <u>zelker</u> (<u>to inspect</u>) is found in the vocabulary lists.

Among the incorrect choices, response A erroneously adds the plural verb form <u>im</u> to the infinitive <u>zelker</u>; response B erroneously uses the verb in its singular form <u>tulem</u>; responses C and D erroneously use the past tense <u>tulzotim</u>; in addition, response D erroneously adds the plural verb ending <u>im</u> to the infinitive <u>zelker</u>.

Question 26   The answer is A: <u>almanleoz trenedlekoz</u>

First, the adjective <u>almanleoz</u> is formed by changing the suffix <u>lek</u> in the noun <u>almanlek</u> (<u>government</u>) to the adjectival suffix <u>le</u>, thus transforming the noun into the adjective <u>almanle</u> (<u>governmental</u>), and then adding the plural suffix <u>oz</u> to the adjective, since adjectives modifying plural nouns must take plural endings (see Rules 10, 3, and 2). ***Second***, the plural noun <u>trenedlekoz</u> (<u>papers</u>) is formed, according to Rule 2, by adding the plural suffix <u>oz</u> to the singular form of the noun.

Among the incorrect choices, responses B and C erroneously use the singular noun <u>almanlek</u> (<u>government</u>) and, in addition, response B also erroneously uses the singular noun <u>trenedlek</u> (<u>paper</u>); response D erroneously uses the plural noun <u>almanlekoz</u> (<u>governments</u>); and response E erroneously uses the singular form of the adjective <u>almanle</u> (<u>governmental</u>).

Question 27   The answer is D: <u>lexlekoz</u>

The plural noun <u>lexlekoz</u> (<u>stations</u>) is formed by first applying Rule 9, according to which in order to form a noun from a verb you should add the suffix <u>lek</u> to the stem of the verb. Then, apply Rule 2, according to which you must add the suffix <u>oz</u> to form the plural of a noun.

Among the incorrect choices, response A incorrectly applies Rule 2 and adds the suffix <u>oz</u> to the infinitive <u>lexker</u>; response B incorrectly applies Rule 12 and adds the possessive suffix <u>ae</u> to the noun <u>lexlek</u>; response C incorrectly applies the possessive suffix <u>ae</u> to the infinitive <u>lexker</u>; and response E incorrectly applies Rule 10 to form the adjectival form <u>lexle</u> instead of the noun <u>lexlek</u>.

Question 28   The answer is A: <u>volle failekae</u>

First, the word <u>volle</u> means <u>this</u> and is found in the vocabulary lists. ***Second***, the word <u>failekae</u> is a possessive form which is formed according to Rule 12 by adding the suffix <u>ae</u> to the noun <u>failek</u> (<u>country</u>), itself found in the vocabulary lists.

Among the incorrect choices, responses B and D erroneously add the possessive <u>ae</u> to the adjective <u>volle</u>; responses C and D erroneously omit the possessive in <u>failek</u>; and response E erroneously uses an adjectival form (<u>faile</u>) instead of the noun <u>failek</u>.

Question 29   The answer is B: <u>janleki bontooz</u>

First, the adverb <u>janleki</u> (<u>skillfully</u>) is formed, according to Rule 11, by adding the suffix <u>ki</u> to the masculine form of the adjective <u>janle</u> (which appears in the vocabulary lists). *Second*, the verb <u>bontooz</u> is in the form of a past participle (<u>guarded</u>). According to Rule 8, the past participle of a verb is formed by adding the suffix <u>to</u> to the stem of the verb. Also, according to Rule 8, when the participle is used as a predicate with the verb <u>to be</u>, it must take the plural form if the noun it modifies is plural.

Among the incorrect choices, responses A and D erroneously add the plural suffix <u>oz</u>, which is NOT used for adverbs; in addition, responses A and D erroneously use the past tense of the verb rather than the participle. Response C uses the correct adverb (<u>janleki</u>), but fails to add the plural ending to the participle. Response E erroneously uses the adverbial ending <u>ki</u> with the noun <u>guard</u> (<u>bonlek</u>), rather than using the participle.

Question 30   The answer is B: <u>vollenefoz inlenefoz kapleknefoz</u>

First, the adjective <u>vollenefoz</u> (<u>these</u>) is formed, according to Rules 3, 1, and 2, by adding the feminine suffix <u>nef</u> and then the plural suffix <u>oz</u> to the masculine singular form (<u>volle</u>). *Second*, the adjective <u>inlenefoz</u> (<u>loyal</u>) is formed, according to the same rules, by adding the same suffixes, <u>nef</u> and <u>oz</u>, to the masculine singular form (<u>inle</u>). *Third*, the noun <u>kapleknefoz</u> (<u>women</u>) is formed, according to Rules 1 and 2, by adding the suffix <u>nef</u> to the masculine noun <u>kaplek</u> (<u>man</u>) and then adding the suffix <u>oz</u> to <u>kapleknef</u> (<u>woman</u>) in order to make it plural.

Among the incorrect choices, responses A and C incorrectly omit the feminine suffix in the adjective <u>volleoz</u>; in addition, response A incorrectly omits the plural suffix in the adjective <u>inlenef</u>, and response C incorrectly omits both the feminine suffix and the plural suffix in the adjective <u>inle</u>. Response D incorrectly omits the plural suffix in the adjective <u>inlenef</u>, and response E incorrectly omits both the feminine suffix and the plural suffix in the adjective <u>inle</u>.

Question 31   The answer is A: <u>ekaplekoz pirzotim</u>
(The sentence <u>Velleoz ekaplekoz pirzotim</u> means <u>Those boys escaped</u>.)

First, the noun <u>ekaplekoz</u> (<u>boys</u>), is formed, according to Rule 2, by adding the suffix <u>oz</u> to the singular form of the noun (<u>ekaplek</u>: <u>boy</u>), which is found in the vocabulary lists. *Second*, the verb <u>pirzotim</u> (<u>escaped</u>) is formed, according to Rules 4 and 7, by first adding the past tense suffix <u>zot</u> to the stem of the verb and then adding the suffix <u>im</u> to denote that the subject of the sentence (and hence the verb) is plural.

Among the incorrect choices, responses B and D erroneously add the plural verb suffix <u>im</u> to the infinitive form of the verb (<u>pirker</u>); in addition, response D erroneously adds the verb suffix <u>im</u> to the noun <u>ekaplek</u> (<u>boy</u>). Response C likewise erroneously adds the verb suffix <u>im</u> to <u>ekaplek</u>. Response E erroneously uses the possessive suffix <u>ae</u> to form the plural of the noun <u>ekaplek</u>.

Question 32   The answer is D: <u>arzotim janleki</u>
(The sentence <u>Wirnefoz kapleknefoz arzotim janleki</u> means <u>The women drove skillfully</u>.)

First, the verb <u>arzotim</u> (<u>drove</u>) is formed, according to Rules 4 and 7, by first adding the past tense suffix <u>zot</u> to the stem of the verb and then adding the suffix <u>im</u> to denote that the subject of the sentence (and hence the verb) is plural. *Second*, the adverb <u>janleki</u> (<u>skillfully</u>) is formed, according to Rule 11, by adding the suffix <u>ki</u> to the masculine form of the adjective. The adjective, <u>janle</u>, is found in the vocabulary lists.

Among the incorrect choices, responses A and B erroneously add the feminine suffix <u>nef</u> to the verb. Similarly, responses A and C erroneously add the feminine suffix to the adverb, and responses B and E erroneously add both the feminine suffix and the plural suffix <u>oz</u> to the adverb (if you refer to Rule 11 you will note that adverbs never take feminine or plural endings).

Question 33   The answer is A: <u>yevnefae kometlek</u>
(The sentence <u>Yevoz liazotim yevnefae kometlek</u> means <u>They injured her friend</u>.)

First, the word <u>yevnefae</u> (<u>her</u>) is formed by successively applying Rules 1 and 12: Rule 1 states that the feminine of a pronoun is formed by adding the suffix <u>nef</u> to the masculine form of the pronoun (accordingly, <u>yev</u> is <u>he</u>, while <u>yevnef</u> is <u>she</u>); Rule 12 states that to form the possessive form of a pronoun (in this case to form <u>her</u>), you should add the suffix <u>ae</u> to the pronoun (thus forming <u>yevnefae</u>). *Second*, the noun <u>kometlek</u> (<u>friend</u>) is found in the vocabulary lists.

Among the incorrect choices, responses B and E erroneously omit the possessive ending for the pronoun <u>yevnef</u> (meaning <u>she</u> rather than <u>her</u>); response C erroneously omits the feminine ending <u>nef</u> for the pronoun (which, as <u>yevae</u>, means <u>his</u>, rather than <u>her</u>); and, finally, responses D and E erroneously add the feminine ending <u>nef</u> to the noun <u>kometlek</u> (<u>friend</u>). In this last case you should note that, according to Rule 1, the feminine ending <u>nef</u> should be added only when the gender is explicitly feminine; in this case the gender of the "friend" is not specified in the sentence and, consequently, the noun <u>friend</u> (<u>kometlek</u>) must remain in the masculine form.

Question 34   The answer is B: <u>Yevnef synzotem</u>
(The sentence <u>Yevnef synzotem mor velle failek</u> means <u>She was from that country</u>.)

First, the pronoun <u>yevnef</u> (<u>she</u>) is formed, according to Rule 1, by adding the feminine suffix <u>nef</u> to the masculine pronoun <u>yev</u> (<u>he</u>). *Second*, the verb <u>synzotem</u> (<u>was</u>) is formed, according to Rules 4 and 7 by first adding the past-tense suffix <u>zot</u> to the stem of the verb and then adding the suffix <u>em</u> to denote that the subject of the sentence (and hence the verb) is singular.

Among the incorrect choices, responses A, C, and E erroneously use the plural suffix <u>im</u> for the verb; response E erroneously omits the past-tense suffix <u>zot</u>, and responses C and D erroneously add the feminine suffix <u>nef</u> to the verb (recall that verbs and adverbs never take feminine endings).

Question 35   The answer is B: kapleknefozae trenedlekoz
(The sentence <u>Wiroz kapleknefozae trenedlekoz synim colleoz</u> means <u>The women's papers are legal</u>.)

First, the plural possessive feminine noun <u>kapleknefozae</u> (<u>women's</u>) is formed by applying, successively, Rule 1 (which forms the feminine <u>kapleknef</u>—<u>woman</u>—by adding the suffix <u>nef</u> to the masculine noun <u>kaplek</u>—<u>man</u>), Rule 2 (which forms the plural <u>kapleknefoz</u>—<u>women</u>—by adding the plural suffix <u>oz</u>), and Rule 12 (which forms the possessive <u>kapleknefozae</u>—<u>women's</u>—by adding the possessive suffix <u>ae</u>). *Second*, the noun <u>trenedlekoz</u> (<u>papers</u>) is formed by adding the plural suffix <u>oz</u> to the word for <u>paper</u>, <u>trenedlek</u> (which is found in the vocabulary lists).

Among the incorrect choices, responses A and C erroneously omit the plural suffix <u>oz</u> in the possessive noun <u>women's</u> (thus making the noun <u>woman's</u> in the possessive singular form); in addition, response C erroneously omits the plural suffix <u>oz</u> in the noun <u>papers</u>, and instead uses the possessive suffix <u>ae</u> (thus making the noun <u>paper's</u> in the possessive singular form). Response D erroneously adds the possessive suffix <u>ae</u> to the noun <u>papers</u> (thus making it into the possessive plural <u>papers'</u>), and response E erroneously makes the noun <u>papers</u> feminine by adding the suffix <u>nef</u> to it.

Question 36   The answer is E: tulem chonker
(The sentence <u>Yevnef tulem chonker velle browlek</u> means <u>She has to cross that river</u>.)

First, the verb <u>tulem</u> (<u>has</u>) is formed, according to Rules 4 and 6, by adding the singular suffix <u>em</u> to the stem of the infinitive <u>tulker</u> (<u>to have</u>). *Second*, the infinitive verb <u>chonker</u> (<u>to cross</u>) is found in the vocabulary lists.

Among the incorrect choices, responses A and B incorrectly add the feminine suffix <u>nef</u> to both verb forms (A gives a different placement to the suffix in the verb <u>has</u>). Response C erroneously adds the singular suffix <u>em</u> to the infinitive <u>chonker</u>. Response D erroneously uses the infinitive form <u>to have</u> (<u>tulker</u>) and then adds the singular suffix <u>em</u> to it.

Question 37   The answer is C: frigim fercolleki
(The sentence <u>Yevoz frigim fercolleki</u> means <u>They work illegally</u>.)

First, since the pronoun <u>yevoz</u> (<u>they</u>) is a plural subject, the present-tense verb <u>work</u> must be plural (Rule 5); it is formed, according to Rules 4 and 6, by adding the suffix <u>im</u> to the stem of the infinitive (which is itself found in the vocabulary lists), thus obtaining <u>frigim</u>. *Second*, the negative adverb <u>illegally</u> is formed, according to Rules 13 and 11, by adding the negative prefix <u>fer</u> to the affirmative form <u>colle</u>—<u>legal</u> (the affirmative form is found in the vocabulary lists), and by adding the adverbial suffix <u>ki</u> to the adjectival form.

Among the incorrect choices, response A erroneously applies the singular suffix <u>em</u> instead of the plural suffix <u>im</u>; response B erroneously omits the negative prefix <u>fer</u> in the adverb; response D erroneously uses the verb suffix <u>im</u> instead of the adverbial suffix <u>ki</u> for the adverb; and response E erroneously uses the verb in the singular (<u>frigem</u>) and erroneously applies the same singular verb ending <u>em</u> to the adverb.

Question 38   The answer is D: <u>tulzotim tatto</u>
(The sentence <u>Wirnefoz ferinlenefoz kapleknefoz tulzotim tatto</u> means <u>The disloyal women had spied</u>.)

First, the word <u>tulker</u> (to have) is found in the vocabulary lists. *Second*, the plural past tense form of <u>tulker</u> is formed, according to Rules 4 and 7, by adding the past tense suffix <u>zot</u> and the plural suffix <u>im</u> to the stem (thus forming the word <u>tulzotim</u>: <u>had</u>). *Third*, the past participle <u>tatto</u> (spied) is formed by adding the suffix <u>to</u> to the stem of the verb <u>tatker</u>, according to Rule 8.

Among the incorrect choices, response A incorrectly uses the infinitive of both <u>tulker</u> and <u>tatker</u>. Responses C and E do not use the plural suffix with <u>tulker</u>, and responses B and C do not use the past tense suffix with <u>tulker</u>. Responses A, B, and E do not use the suffix <u>to</u> with <u>tatker</u>. In addition, response C incorrectly uses the past participle of <u>tatker</u> as an adjective.

Question 39   The answer is A: <u>Velle almanlekae tatlekoz</u>
(The sentence <u>Velle almanlekae tatlekoz synzotim avelekoz</u> means <u>That government's spies were enemies</u>.)

First, the word <u>velle</u> (<u>that</u>) is found in the vocabulary lists. *Second*, the possessive form of the noun <u>almanlek</u> (<u>government</u>) is formed, according to Rule 12, by adding the suffix <u>ae</u> to the noun (thus forming the word <u>almanlekae</u>: <u>government's</u>). *Third*, the plural noun <u>tatlekoz</u> (<u>spies</u>) is formed by adding the suffix <u>oz</u> to the singular form of the noun <u>tatlek</u> (which is itself formed, according to Rules 4 and 9, by adding the suffix <u>lek</u> to the stem of the infinitive).

Among the incorrect choices, responses C, D, and E use the wrong word for <u>that</u>—the correct word is <u>velle</u>, not <u>volle</u>, which means <u>this</u>. In addition, responses D and E erroneously add the plural suffix <u>oz</u> to the noun <u>almanlek</u> (<u>government</u>), and response E erroneously omits the possessive form from the noun. Response B similarly omits the possessive form <u>ae</u> and erroneously adds the plural suffix <u>oz</u>.

Question 40   The answer is E: <u>fersynem bexnef fercollenef</u>
(The sentence <u>Yevnef fersynem bexnef fercollenef husleknef</u> means <u>She is not an illegal alien</u>.)

First, the verb <u>fersynem</u> (<u>is not</u>) is formed according to Rules 4, 6, and 13: According to Rules 4 and 6, the singular form of the verb is formed by adding the singular suffix <u>em</u> to the stem of the infinitive (thus <u>synem</u>); and according to Rule 13, the negative form of the verb, <u>is not</u>, is formed by adding the prefix <u>fer</u> to the affirmative form (thus <u>fersynem</u>). *Second*, the article <u>bex</u> (<u>a/an</u>), as stated in Rules 1 and 3, takes the feminine ending <u>nef</u> to agree in gender with the noun it modifies. *Third*, the negative adjective <u>fercollenef</u> is formed, according to Rules 1 and 13, by adding the feminine suffix <u>nef</u> to the masculine form of the adjective (according to Rule 3, when an adjective is modifying a feminine noun, as is the case here, it must take a feminine ending), and by adding the negative prefix <u>fer</u> to the affirmative form (thus, <u>fercollenef</u>).

Among the incorrect choices, response A erroneously omits the feminine suffix from the adjective. Responses B erroneously omits the feminine ending from the article bex. Response C erroneously omits the feminine ending from the adjective. Response D erroneously translates the sentence into affirmative form (by omitting the negative suffix from both the verb and the adjective) and erroneously omits the feminine suffix from the adjective.

Question 41   The answer is B: bonlekae lexlek fercolleki
(The complete sentence Yev chonzotem wir bonlekae lexlek fercolleki means He crossed the guard's station illegally.)

First, the possessive noun bonlekae (guard's) is formed according to Rules 4, 9, and 12 by first adding the nominal suffix lek to the stem of the infinitive (itself found in the vocabulary lists), thus obtaining the noun bonlek (guard), and then adding the possessive suffix ae to the noun. *Second*, the noun lexlek (station) is formed according to Rules 4 and 9 by adding the nominal suffix lek to the stem of the infinitive (itself found in the vocabulary lists). *Third*, the negative adverb fercolleki is formed, according to Rules 11 and 13, by adding the adverbial suffix ki to the masculine form of the adjective, and by adding the negative prefix fer to the affirmative form of the word.

Among the incorrect choices, responses A and C incorrectly add the singular verb suffix em to the noun bonlek; in addition, response C adds this suffix to the noun lexlek. Response D erroneously omits the possessive suffix ae from the noun bonlek, and response E erroneously adds this suffix to the noun lexlek and to the adverb.

Question 42   The answer is E: zeltooz
(The sentence Wiroz zeltooz kaplekoz chonzotim wir reglek means The inspected men crossed the border.)

First, the past participle zelto (inspected) is formed according to Rule 8 by adding the suffix to to the stem of the verb. **Second**, because the past participle is used as an adjective to modify the plural masculine noun men, the plural suffix oz is added to the past participle zelto, thus forming zeltooz.

Among the incorrect choices, responses A, B, and D do not form the past participle. Although response C forms the past participle, the past participle does not agree in number with noun it modifies.

Question 43   The answer is C: tulim chonto
(The sentence Wiroz huslekoz tulim chonto wir browlek means The aliens have crossed the river.)

According to the instructions in parentheses, the compound verb must be in the present perfect plural form. Therefore, according to Rule 8, the suffix im must be added to the stem of tulker in order to make it present tense, and the suffix to must be added to the stem of chonker to form the past participle.

Among the incorrect choices, response A does not use the past participle form of <u>chonker</u>. Response B incorrectly uses the past participle form of <u>tulker</u>. In responses D and E, the past tense of <u>tulker</u> is used incorrectly. Also, in responses B and E, the incorrect plural form of the participle is used.

Question 44   The answer is B: <u>ferinlenefoz</u>
(The sentence <u>Yevnefoz fersynim ferinlenefoz</u> means <u>They</u> (fem.) <u>are not disloyal.</u>)

According to the instructions in parentheses, the adjective <u>inle</u> (loyal) must be in the negative plural feminine form. Therefore, according to Rule 13, the negative prefix <u>fer</u> must be added to <u>inle</u>. Then, according to Rules 3, 1, and 2, the suffix <u>nef</u> must be added to the masculine form in order to make it feminine, and, subsequently, the suffix <u>oz</u> must be added to form the plural.

Among the incorrect choices, response A erroneously uses <u>fer</u> as a suffix and omits both the feminine and the plural suffixes; response C omits the plural; responses D and E omit the feminine; and response E is misspelled (the letter <u>n</u> is meaningless relative to the adjacent components of the word: <u>inle</u> and <u>oz</u>).

Question 45   The answer is B: <u>arzotem—janleki</u>
(The sentence <u>Yevnef arzotem janleki mor wir lexlek</u> means <u>She drove skillfully from the station.</u>)

According to the instructions in parentheses, the verb (<u>arker</u>) must be in the past tense, and the adjective (<u>janle</u>) must be converted to adverbial form. In the case of the verb, the past tense singular is formed by adding the past-tense suffix <u>zot</u> to the stem of the infinitive and then adding the singular suffix <u>em</u> after <u>zot</u> (Rules 4 and 7). In the case of the adverb, according to Rule 11, an adverb is formed by adding the suffix <u>ki</u> to the masculine form of the adjective. You should recall in this context that verbs and adverbs never take feminine endings and that adverbs do not take plural endings.

Among the incorrect choices, responses A and D erroneously add the feminine suffix to the verb; responses C, D, and E erroneously add the feminine suffix to the adverb; and response C altogether omits the adverbial ending <u>ki</u>, thus forming a feminine adjective (<u>janlenef</u>) rather than an adverb.

Question 46   The answer is A: <u>Vollenefoz—kapleknefozae</u>
(The sentence <u>Vollenefoz kapleknefozae trenedlekoz synzotim mor yevnefae failek</u> means <u>These women's papers were from her country.</u>)

According to the instructions in parentheses, the adjective <u>these</u> is a feminine plural adjective (since it must agree with the plural feminine noun <u>women</u> according to Rule 3). Therefore, according to Rules 1 and 2, the adjective <u>volle</u> must take the feminine suffix <u>nef</u> followed by the plural suffix <u>oz</u>. In regard to the noun, the instructions say that it is a feminine plural possessive noun. First, according to Rules 1 and 2, the feminine suffix <u>nef</u> is added to <u>kaplek</u>, followed by the plural ending <u>oz</u>. Finally, the possessive suffix <u>ae</u> is added (Rule 12).

Among the incorrect response choices, response B erroneously adds the feminine suffix after the plural suffix. This procedure violates Rules 1 and 2, which state that the feminine singular is formed by adding the feminine suffix to the masculine singular and that the plural of nouns is formed by adding the plural suffix <u>oz</u> to the correct <u>singular</u> form. Response C altogether omits the use of the feminine suffix in the adjective and the use of the plural suffix in the noun. Response D omits the possessive suffix in the noun; and response E erroneously adds the possessive suffix to the singular form of the noun (and then, meaninglessly, adds the plural suffix to this possessive singular).

Question 47   The answer is E: <u>zelleknefoz—yevnefoz</u>
(The sentence <u>Wirnefoz kapleknefoz synzotim zelleknefoz, loa yevnefoz degzotim wir tatlek</u> means <u>The women were inspectors, and they shot the spy</u>.)

According to the instructions in parentheses, both the noun (derived from <u>zelker</u>) and the pronoun (<u>yev</u>) must be in the feminine plural form. First, the noun <u>zellek</u> is formed from the verb <u>zelker</u> according to rules 4 and 9. Then, according to Rule 1, the suffix <u>nef</u> must be added to the singular masculine noun <u>zellek</u> before adding the plural suffix <u>oz</u>. In the case of the pronoun, exactly the same rule applies and, therefore, the suffix <u>nef</u> must be added to the singular pronoun <u>yev</u> (<u>he</u>) before adding the plural suffix <u>oz</u>.

Among the incorrect response choices, responses A and C omit the feminine suffix from the noun, and response C also omits it from the pronoun; responses B and D erroneously add the plural suffix to the infinitive verb <u>zelker</u>, rather than to the noun <u>zellek</u>, and, in addition, they both omit the feminine suffix from the noun (with response D also omitting it from the pronoun).

Question 48   The answer is A: <u>aveleknef—kalentonef</u>
(The sentence <u>Wirnef aveleknef synzotem kalentonef</u> means <u>The enemy</u> (feminine) <u>was identified</u>.)

According to the instructions in parentheses, both the noun (<u>avelek</u>) and the past participle (from <u>kalenker</u>) must be in the feminine singular form. In the case of the noun, according to Rule 1, the suffix <u>nef</u> must be added to the singular masculine noun <u>avelek</u>. In the case of the past participle, according to rules 4 and 8, the suffix <u>to</u> must be added to the stem <u>kalen</u> before adding the feminine suffix <u>nef</u>.

Among the incorrect response choices, responses C and E omit the feminine suffix from the noun, and response C also omits it from the past participle; responses B, D, and E fail to form the past participle. In addition, response C omits the feminine suffix from the past participle.

Question 49   The answer is D: <u>fercollenefoz—husleknefozae—deglekoz</u>
(The sentence <u>Vellenefoz fercollenefoz husleknefozae deglekoz liazotim wiroz ekaplekoz</u> means <u>Those illegal aliens' (fem.) shots injured the boys</u>.)

According to the instructions in parentheses, the first word to be formed is the negative feminine plural adjective <u>fercollenefoz</u> (<u>illegal</u>). The negative adjective is formed according to Rule 13 by adding the prefix <u>fer</u> to the affirmative form (<u>colle</u>); the feminine plural is formed according to

Rules 3, 1, and 2 by adding the feminine suffix <u>nef</u> to the masculine form and then adding the plural suffix <u>oz</u> to the feminine form. The second word to be formed is the possessive feminine plural noun <u>husleknefozae</u> (<u>aliens'</u>). This noun is formed by adding, consecutively, the feminine suffix <u>nef</u>, the plural suffix <u>oz</u>, and the possessive suffix <u>ae</u> to the singular masculine noun <u>huslek</u>. The third word to be formed is the plural noun <u>deglekoz</u> (<u>shots</u>). This noun is formed according to Rules 9 and 2 by adding the suffix <u>lek</u> to the stem (<u>deg</u>) of the infinitive verb <u>degker</u> (<u>to shoot</u>), and then adding the plural suffix <u>oz</u> to the noun (thus, <u>deglekoz</u>).

Among the incorrect choices, response A erroneously omits the plural suffix <u>oz</u> in the adjective and both the feminine suffix <u>nef</u> and the plural suffix <u>oz</u> in the possessive noun. Response B erroneously omits the feminine suffix <u>nef</u> and the plural suffix <u>oz</u> in both the adjective and the possessive noun. Response C erroneously omits the feminine suffix <u>nef</u> in the adjective and the plural suffix <u>oz</u> in both the adjective and the possessive noun. Response E erroneously adds the feminine suffix <u>nef</u> to the noun <u>deglekoz</u> (<u>shots</u>), whose gender is not specified and must therefore be masculine.

Question 50   The answer is B: <u>liatooz—ferkometleoz</u>
(The sentence <u>Wiroz liatooz ekaplekoz synzotim ferkometleoz</u> means <u>The injured boys were unfriendly</u>.)

According to the instructions in parentheses, the first word to be formed is the plural past participle adjective <u>liatooz</u> (<u>injured</u>). According to Rule 8, the past participle must agree in number and gender with <u>ekaplekoz</u>, the noun which the adjectival past participle modifies. The past participle is formed according to Rules 4 and 8 by adding the suffix <u>to</u> to the stem <u>lia</u>. The plural participle is formed by adding the suffix <u>oz</u>. The second word to be formed is the negative plural adjective <u>ferkometleoz</u> (<u>unfriendly</u>). The adjective <u>kometle</u> is formed from the noun <u>kometlek</u> according to Rule 10. The negative prefix <u>fer</u> and the plural suffix <u>oz</u> are then added, according to Rules 13 and 2.

Among the incorrect choices, responses A and D fail to form the past participle. Although response C correctly forms the past participle, the participle in response C is singular. Responses A and E fail to negate the predicate, while response C fails to use the plural form of the predicate.

www.ingramcontent.com/pod-product-compliance
Lightning Source LLC
Chambersburg PA
CBHW081115280526
45787CB00007B/2845